THE CHILDREN'S BREAD

Accessing Faith-based Economics and Personal Wealth By Unlocking Whole Life Stewardship

Hollis L. Green

GREEN WINE
FAMILY BOOKS

THE CHILDREN'S BREAD

**Accessing Faith-based Economics and Personal Wealth
By Unlocking Whole Life Stewardship**

Copyright © 2018 by Hollis L. Green

Library of Congress Control Number: 2018913115

Green, Hollis L., 1933 –

THE CHILDREN'S BREAD
Accessing Faith-based Economics and Personal Wealth
By Unlocking Whole Life Stewardship

ISBN 978-1-935434-90-0 Print

ISBN 978-1-935434-98-6 eBook

Subject Codes and Description: 1: REL 063000: Religion: Christian Life
– Stewardship & Giving 2: REL 006100 Religion: Biblical Criticism & Inter-
pretation –New Testament 3: BUS 074010 Business & Economics/ Nonprofit
Organizations & Charities/Finance & Accounting

Cover by Global Graphics, NYC

Printed in Australia, Brazil, France, Germany, Italy, Poland, Spain, EU,
UK and USA and available on the Espresso Book Machine©

Order books from www.gea-books.com/bookstore/

or any place good books are sold.

Published by

GreenWine Family Books™

A division of GlobalEdAdvancePress

Dedication

This work is dedicated, with affection,
To the participants of

THE LEARNING CENTRE
New Life Baptist Church
Bluff City, TN

A venue where the original syllabus
Of this book was first taught.

"Wealth Magnifies Character
— Who you are without money multiplies
with each added dollar."

BARTON L. GREEN

"A philanthropist is anyone who gives
anything — time, money, experience,
skills, and networks— in any amount to
create a better world."

— LAURA ARRILLAGA-ANDEESSEN
from GIVING 2.0 (2012)

Contents

First, we must unlock kingdom thinking about prosperity and God's user-friendly approach to wealth found in His Sixty-six (66) book library. The entry card is free but requires effort to find the needed data and learn to properly use the knowledge.

Foreword

Dr. Green has delivered fresh insights through **THE CHILDREN'S BREAD** --*Accessing Faith-based Economics and Personal Wealth By Unlocking Whole Life Stewardship.* Skillfully he navigates through Old and New Testament scriptures, influences from his upbringing and personal experiences to produce a beautiful narration. The book offers guidance, hope and encouragement to all who are struggling with money-management issues, and are genuinely yearning to get a handle on effective financial stewardship.

As you read this book, you would observe that the author writes from a heart of 'steel and velvet.' On the steel side, he is unflinching in his statements. You would be introduced to concepts such as *"Kingdom Thinking and Kingdom Economics;" "Green and Brown money;" "Spiritual and Sweat Equity."* You would also meet bold statements, such as *"The lack of knowledge of how financial matters work is inexcusable;" "We must unlock kingdom thinking about prosperity;" "Discipline in money matters;" "Money (and everything) is about the Future."* However, on the velvet side of the narrative, Dr. Green is compassionate in his counsel and guidance. You would get the feeling that he is actually walking alongside you, the reader, to escort you out of the distresses associated with financial ignorance and the tyranny of financial deception.

The book essentially targets the children of the Kingdom enterprise, and speaks directly to individuals, parents, families and leaders of faith-based institutions…especially those who are faced with ongoing crises of lack and appear to set their address permanently under the 'liabilities column' of the weekly balance sheet. Still, these persons silently long to crossover and change address to the 'assets column.' Dr. Green offers guidance and thus is a 'must-have!' It presents all-time, liberating scriptural and pragmatic nuggets that are sure to cause you to cry out, *"I can see clearly now!"* The book is reasonably priced for the widest access. Don't miss this opportunity to own your personal copy and begin reading your way through the gateway to responsible and profitable financial stewardship. I can assure you that the small investment you would make delivers enormous returns. —**Pastor Lewin Mayer**, PhD

Queen's Royal College; OASIS Institute of Higher Learning

FIRST READER REVIEWS

Reviews from the first readers of the draft manuscript of **THE CHILDREN'S BREAD** --*Accessing Faith-based Economics and Personal Wealth By Unlocking Whole Life Stewardship:*

Readers will appreciate the author's breadth and depth of experience in operations of the Church and civil society. He presents economic growth and development as practiced in both spheres and clearly identifies principles imperative for God-based growth and development. Two areas impact greatly: honest labor and being "givers." While the opposite of these two constructs are workable with rewards in an adversarial kingdom or "worldly" environment, they bear no fruit in God's economic processes.

The author strongly emphasizes the concept of *"by the sweat of your brow"* and his early indoctrination to this truth. This is a principle for achievement for the majority with no shortcuts or alternatives. Migration from being "takers" to becoming "givers" results in abundance and equitable distribution with adequate resources to finance the objectives of God. This book is a must read for audiences aspiring to become disciples.

Paratan Balloo, MBA, DPhil, *a Fellow in the Oxford Society of Scholars with a background in business, education, finance, and religion, he leads OASIS UNIVERSITY as Vice Chancellor/CEO, but remains involved in wealth management and financial services. His most recent book: Leadership Theory & Social Change.*

Most of us lack a true Biblical understanding of financial management. We do not know the principles for gaining, saving, or spending. Too many of us use the abundance which God gives us on personal possessions rather than on advancing the Kingdom. This book identifies these principles, explains in detail those words and terms, and espouses living within the means the Father provides. Both clergy and laity will benefit from reading this book; it provides a clear, concise, consistent, and correct view of Kingdom finances both for individuals and congregations of the Body of Christ. I strongly recommend the reading and study of this book.

Donald B. Smith, MSSW, DPhil, LCSW Board Certified Diplomate in Clinical Social Work; Director, Christian Missionary Evangelism. Dr. Smith was the first Board Certified Clinical Social Worker in the United States in the field of geriatrics. His most recent textbook, Living with a Dead Battery is a detailed review of the different types of depression and the available interventions.

Our giving to God is not a debt we owe, but a seed we sow. God has given each one the ability to create wealth; however, we must be prudent in the distribution of funds. We must ensure that we are creating impactful results. Not all projects presented for funding are suitable to meet our sphere of expertise and influence. One must also have a good report on the persons or group requesting funding and their ability to manage their own finances and make informed decisions to ensure continuity. Before a donation, I usually ask two questions: *Can the project withstand the present and future situation? How will the risk factors and concerns be managed?*

Subesh Ramjattan, DHL, DLitt, a leader in philanthropy and business development and consistent support of missions and faith-based causes. A successful entrepreneur with a proven track record for building and operating businesses based on sound ethics, governance practices, and social responsibility. Presently serving as Managing Director, The House of Marketing, Ltd. a company he founded in 1976. His most recent book: Ageing Has a Silver Lining: 2nd Edition

It was a joy to read the manuscript of your up-coming book: **THE CHILDREN'S BREAD** --*Accessing Faith-based Economics and Personal Wealth By Unlocking Whole Life Stewardship.* The broad approach to unlocking a Missional Lifestyle and funding for Faith-based operations was supported with both data and explanation. It conveyed the heart of inclusivity to all humanity designed by the Everlasting God. Such is in line with Pau's sentiments expressed in Romans 15:7, *Receive those whom the Lord has received.* Such instructions from the apostle and your manuscript are in complete harmony. Congratulations, for achieving *Hashem's* Heart (God's heart) in this work and may the transcending *Shalom* of *YHWH* be with you and each of your readers. *Shalom.*

Rabbi Oswald Garagorry, DPhil, *President of Yeshiva Torah Institute and Rabbi of Aliyah Congregation, who is establishing a bridging framework from the past to the present to gather Jewish converts into a lifelong learning exposure to the entire Word of God.*

Dr. Green has provided practical guidance for implementing Biblical instructions and why we should live by those principles. Anyone striving to live according to Christian financial principles has to first understand them. Jesus spoke a great deal about money; therefore, it is important that we follow His teaching. I would recommend that anyone wanting to become a better steward of the resources God provided to read **THE CHILDREN'S BREAD** --*Accessing Faith-based Economics and Personal Wealth By Unlocking Whole Life Stewardship.*

Businessman Jerry Fleming, *MLitt, DPhil, with a background in Industrial and Mechanical Engineering and owner of Pioneer Mfg. Inc. and present CEO of THE STEM FOUNDATION. His doctoral research focused on the relationship between "morality and the earnings of publicly held companies."*

In **THE CHILDREN'S BREAD** --*Accessing Faith-based Economics and Personal Wealth By Unlocking Whole Life Stewardship,* Dr. Green provides believers with a tremendous challenge. It is a challenge to modern day materialistic society and the subjective stress many people face in the realm of finances. This book is a reminder that lasting legacies, families, and ministries are built on things of eternal nature and value rather than on the temporal things of this world. Believer's must have a mindset on the things above so they become true missionaries in lifestyle and consequent actions. Doing this, we are able to take seats at the table and capitalize on the blessings God has promised while actively supporting the Kingdom with a missional lifestyle. This is a much needed challenge for believers and faith-based ministries in this day!

Pastor Coy Webb, MBA, ThD, *Tennessee Tech U; ATSeminary*

I am the Bread of Life. Your fathers did
eat manna in the wilderness, and are
dead. This is the Bread which comes down
from heaven, that a man may eat thereof,
and not die. I am the living Bread which
came down from heaven: if any man eat
of this Bread, he shall live forever:

(John 6:48-51 EDNT)

Prologue

Unlocking a Missional Lifestyle and Funding for Faith-based Entities

This book is based on a lifetime of working with faith-based entities, mission groups, educational institutions and charities structured to enhance an environment conductive to moral living and basic provisions for family, community and the sociological integration of religion and society. In most of the world, there is a common desire for security and basic family and community development. Faith-based entities normally work to produce, protect and preserve individuals in the context of their basic institutions. Although history, language and culture are different, the basic problems of establishing a home, raising a family, educating children, leaving a legacy, developing a stable government, and supporting good and worthy projects are common objectives.

This work is a reaction to the lack of financial understanding among parents, families, and leaders of faith-based entities, about how financial matters actually work. Consequently, there is a failure to adequately fund families and faith-based operations. This appears to be a lack of theoretical or practical grasp of the basic principles and practices utilized historically in the Old and New Testaments to support positive social change and create an environment conducive to the primary work of individuals in a stable family unit.

The author assumes the basis for marriage was to protect the community from immorality and provide a secure place for the birth and education of children. The common objective is for children to become moral citizens of the world and ultimately mystical citizens of a heavenly kingdom. Without sufficient financial knowledge to adequately support themselves and their families, they turn to secular and materialistic sources for guidance. Sadly, the advice and counsel normally benefit the advisors more than the individual, family or the institutions of which they are a part. The incentives to spend, borrow, and take unnecessary risk in an effort to get rich, cripples many who are unprepared for the real world of economics and personal wealth.

Notwithstanding an exposure to historical sources, the author personally discovered principles from sacred writings that appeared to work better for average folk. Some practical lessons and structured data were gathered over the years that should be shared with the common man and his family. This work is an attempt to pass some of that information to families and faith-based entities.

Some subject-related books are in the reference bibliography, but many of the normal guides to best practices for corporate and personal finance are missing. There are policies and practical "ways and means" books designed to assist the working public with their financial arrangements, but many are too poor to pay attention or utilize the assistance available. Perhaps this happens because they lack a foundation for financial management. Meanwhile, the media, sales marketing, and pressure sales push many to live beyond their means and they remain in debt most of their lives. This was expressed in Tennessee Ernie Ford's lyrics, *"Another day older and deeper in debt, St. Peter don't call me 'cause I can't go, I owe my soul to the company store!"* This has become the plight of the poor and the uninformed public. Faith-based institutions could solve part of this problem if they were honestly providing spiritual and practical guidance to their congregants.

The desire to do honest work for honest pay and provide for basic family needs, assist others, participate in the support of faith-based endeavors, and leave a legacy for their children is common in both head and heart for most people regardless of religion or socioeconomic status. This is prevalent across many strata of income, education, culture and occupation. The author assumes that faith-based entities have personal, spiritual and relationship difficulties at the family level rather than financial or budget problems. Consequently, families and places of worship and other faith-based entities have financial shortfalls and problems of debt. Missing is the basic knowledge of *"how things work"* in the personal and financial arena; it is assumed that Faith-based entities could fill this knowledge gap and guide families to a better life. In the process they would improve their capacity and potential for advancing the ethical and spiritual cause of a moral society.

When believers are walking in fellowship with God and others, living in stable family structures, and are taught essential financial practices from sacred writings, sufficient funds are available for family support and the humanitarian and religious work at hand. The author made these assumptions by depending heavily on a general truth, *"Where God guides, He provides!"* Consequently, this book uses sacred scripture, common sense, and practical knowledge from personal experience working with charitable, faith-based groups and educational institutions during the past sixty (60) years.

This work is directed to the many honest, hardworking folk who are willing to do honest work for an honest dollar, but lack spending and planning discipline which makes them vulnerable to a mistaken belief they can borrow enough to get out of debt. Not having the basic knowledge of personal finances was a hard lesson learned early in life. The recognition of the value of planning was slow in coming. My grandfather taught me a short and simple truth about the use of money: "***When your outgo is more than your income; your upkeep is your downfall.***" When I paid attention to this general truth, I usually had a little left after the offering basket and paying bills.

November 1, 2018
Evergreen Cottage
Hollis L. Green, ThD, PhD, DLitt
Morning Air Estate at Lone Mountain
345 Barton Road, Dayton, TN 37321

I

Recognizing
The Value Of Planning

Lack of Basic Financial Knowledge

While studying in a major seminary, a professor explained his tithing practice in class. He announced with great pride that he had "***increased his tithe to 3% on his adjusted gross income.***" Previously his tithe had been 2%; now it was to be an exorbitant 3% on his **adjusted** gross income. Abruptly, a student stood and said, "*Sir, I believe tithe means ten (10) percent – and he held out both hands for the class to see 10 fingers!*" When a student felt compelled to correct a professor's understand on tithing, it was obvious that the lack of knowledge of whole life stewardship was inexcusable. Especially when he thought 3% *was exceeding the bound of custom, propriety, and reason!* Tragically it was a church growth class filled with pastors and young men preparing for the ministry.

There is a Difference

There is a significant difference between the riches, wealth, and prosperity expressed in the Old Testament and the blessings of the righteous and support for kingdom outreach in the New Testament.

The difficulty was how does one glean from sacred writings the values, principles, standards, sources, antecedents, rules, and guidelines for behavior and handling property, people, and prosperity? What assumptions could be made about the relevance of scripture compared with modern literature on the subject? How does one deal with materialistic philosophy of modern finance while considering the unconventional principles of inspired scripture? This work deals with the difference.

Marketing Techniques Confuse

Modern marketing methods confuse the buyer and sales techniques and technology encourage individuals to purchase things they do not need and cannot afford. Buying is explained as a way to save and bargain sales exhibit direct savings as an incentive to buy now. Advertising techniques are so compelling that it becomes difficult not to buy now. Willie Gayle, my friend who wrote an original Dale Carnegie sales course wrote, *"At the moment someone buys something they do not need or do not want, they are momentarily insane."* The, "but wait" technique, "Order now and you will get a second one absolutely free: just pay a special fee plus shipping and handling." This is no bargain. A bargain is supposed to be low-priced, reduced cost, inexpensive, and a good purchase. Tragically, this is not normally the case.

"But Wait" Technique

This technique was used by Jesus in His Challenge to Believers, which some call the Great

Commission of the church. Jesus was clearly speaking to His followers, "As you personally go into all the world, "wait until the Holy Spirit equips you with power, then as you journey make disciples! Believers by faith make a clear decision to follow the road less traveled and after this need a decision to "wait" for the leadership and enablement of the Spirit. The Spirit comes to believers as a *paraclete (referring in English as the Holy Spirit) defined as "an advocate, comforter, guide at the Believer's side as they journey to make disciples." However, the "but wait" has become delay and procrastination and the process of "going" has become a snail's crawl and little is done because there was a failure to develop a missional lifestyle. This is similar to what happens when one falls under the spell of marketing techniques and waste time, money and gather many things they do no need to operate their lives. This also happens when believers procrastinate.*

Does Shopping save Money?

My wife shops and believes she saves money. After 25 years using the same bank before retirement, I calculated that she had saved $376,014.24. I was certain she had put the savings into a special account to draw interest. At retirement, I went to the President of the bank and said, "According to my calculation, my wife saved $376,014.24 while she shopped during the past 25 years. Since we only use this bank, I came to check on that special savings account with the added interest. With brief puzzlement on his face, the banker said, "Mr. Green you have a little money in this

bank, but nothing that would amount to that figure."
So, I said jokingly, "Just checking, my wife said she
saved the money all these years. I thought it would be
in this bank drawing interest. I had planned to cash it
in and pay off all my debts and go fishing." Then we
both had a good laugh.

Caretakers of Divine Assets

Since all wealth flows from divine provision, a
major function of believers is to be a levelheaded
and trustworthy steward of resources provided
by Providence. Believing God to be the source
of prosperity, the receiver of these benefits is
designated as caretaker of the assets and will be
held accountable for their whole life stewardship.
All disbursement of funds whether for family, legacy,
charity, or current support for kingdom work must be
seen as an investment in the extension of God's will.
It is necessary to follow guidelines in sacred scripture
to be worthy of additional blessings and be accounted
trustworthy of faithful whole life stewardship. To be a
wise steward is a privilege and a responsibility. The
value of stewardship is not gaged by the amount of
money handled, but the manner in which financial
matters are approached and executed. God not
only trust believers with funds for their family and
resources for charity and a legacy to advance God's
will on earth. He permits believers to manage those
funds which support the ongoing plan of God for
mankind through faithful individuals chosen for His
service.

Mature Guidance

An aging Apostle Peter, as he faced the end of his earthly journey, reminded converts and fellow believers of valuable information he wanted them to remember. He included that the Father had fully equipped Jesus for His ministry and that His followers were endowed by the Holy Spirit with power and resources to continue and complete His mission to the world following the guidance of sacred scripture.

12. It is for these reasons that I intend to constantly remind you of these things, although you know them well, and are grounded firmly in the present truth. 13. I think it right, as long as I am living, to refresh your memory; 14. the Lord Jesus Christ has showed me that shortly I must fold my tent. 15. Moreover, **I will make it my endeavor that after my departure you will always remember these things.** *16. For we have not pursued deceitfully developed allegories but were eyewitnesses to His majesty when He made known to us the power and presence of our Lord Jesus Christ. 17. For He received from God the Father honor (power/ resources) and glory, when a voice came from the magnificent glory This is My Son, My beloved in whom I am delighted. 18. And* **we His companions on the holy mountain heard this voice coming from heaven. 19. So this makes the word of the prophets more certain for us:** *and you do well taking heed, as to a lamp shining in a gloomy place, until the day dawns and the morning star shines in your hearts;* **20. Knowing this firstly, that no prophecy of scripture becomes its own solution. 21. For no prophecy was brought forth by the will of man at any time: but men spoke** *from God being brought forth by the Holy Spirit.* (2 Peter 1:12-21 EDNT)

The Value of Scripture

The aging Paul wrote to young Timothy about the value of scripture as a resource for guidance in all aspects of life. In this same vain my paternal grandfather shared his philosophy of personal finances in one of our long exchanges about life and living. He was a dedicated Methodist believer who read five (5) chapters in the Bible each day for guidance. Speaking slowly and clearly, I knew it was important: *When your outgo is more than your income, your upkeep is your downfall!* These soft words screamed the need for a planning process in personal and family spending. Paul's words to Timothy were longer and covered more territory including that ministers needed to be fully equipped for their sacred occupation.

> *14. But continue to hold fast the things you have learned and been convinced of, knowing the teachers from whom you learned them; 15. and from early childhood you have known the sacred letters, the ones able to make you wise unto salvation through faith in Christ Jesus.* **16. All sacred writings are God-breathed, and serviceable for teaching, for warning, for correction, for guidance in righteousness, 17. in order that the man of God may be adequately equipped for every good work.** (2 Timothy 3:14-17 EDNT)

Baker's Dozen from my Memory Basket

Common sense is worth dollars; plus, added coinage value that is attributed by God.   All income must be divided into expense and savings. Avoid any behavior or action that could cause unexpected expenses: such as, traffic tickets, overdrafts, breakage of equipment or loss or neglect of property. 9. **Honor the Lord** with your wealth, **with the first fruits of all your income; 10. then your storehouses will be filled to overflowing, and your containers will overflow with new wine.** (Proverbs 3:9-10 EDOT) Here is an additional baker's dozen of things I remember about money matters and financial asset management. At age 85, I am unable to cite sources, perhaps it is simply common sense mined from a lifetime of learning:

1. Reserve 10% first for Kingdom matters.

2. Purchase what you need; save for what you want.

3. Spend less than you make; use the overage for others.

4. Use cash and avoid credit; evade incentives to borrow.

5. Extend your income by realistic budget planning; stick to it.

6. Seek scriptural guidance before buying big-ticket items.

7. Use any special connection to purchase for less.

8. Do not hire someone to do services you can provide.

9. Use discretionary spending only as donations to advance the Kingdom.

10. Investments in Kingdom issues are safe in Heavens Bank.

11. Consider a dollar saved as a dollar earned with added interest: permit the dollar to work for you!

12. When funds are received, deposit some in checking and some in savings for future needs. Do not spend funds you need later.

13. Strategic giving stretches income; gifts are measured by the cost to the giver; therefore, share within your means and the divinely calculated coinage value will be increased sufficiently for the need at hand. Remember, Jesus valued the two small coins of the widow were worth more than all the funds presented to the Temple by the wealthy.

Secular Advice vs Scriptural Guidance

A young pastor dropped out of a graduate program designed to improve his ministry. When asked why, his explanation was "man-made and unbiblical." It seems that a Certified Public Accountant had been elected as Treasurer of the church. This young CPA looked at the budget and divided it by the number of members. Then he projected a new expansion budget that would need 50 new members based on the present *per capita* giving. You guessed it: the CPA suggested based on the present "**average per person giving**," the pastor should drop out of his graduate program and concentrate on seeking fifty (50) new members to support the new budget. This placed a "price" on new converts and tied new members to the budget. Instead of encouraging the pastor to seek scriptural guidance and bring existing membership into compliance with God's Word, they simply accepted secular advice on budgeting and abandoned the guidance of sacred scripture. A reasonable growth budget is a good thing, but it should not supersede additional training for the pastor or guidance from the Word of God.

Unwilling Participant

Under such situations those attending group functions feel they have done God a service, when in reality they have only been an unwilling participant in a scheduled activity. The Creator provided lessons to teach individuals and institutions ways and means to disassemble existing programs and find a solution to their limitations. If there is effort to renew the vision and see community outreach opportunities, divine assistance is available because God assists those who are willing to work and support themselves and share with others. **The requirement of physical work for daily bread issued by God in the Garden has not been rescinded.** God's provision of "daily bread" is not an entitlement for lazy folk; it is a divine plan for labor to support family, friends, and the financial means to advance kingdom enterprises. God blesses His people, so they may bless others.

Paul explained how the Word would make believers strong and provide an inheritance among those who were consecrated. He demonstrated his willing participation in hard work and the benefit of giving by paying forward God's blessings.

32. And now, brethren, I commend you to God, and to the Word of His grace, which is able to make you strong, and give you an inheritance among the consecrated ones. 33. I have never asked for silver or gold or clothing from anyone. 34. **You have seen yourself that these hands have supplied not only my own needs, but for the people with me.** *35. In all things, I gave you an example of working hard and that one must provide for the poor. Remember the words of the Lord Jesus, when He said,* **It is more blessed to give than to receive.** (Acts 20:32-35 EDNT)

The Big Question

The big question: how is the "giver" more blessed than the "receiver." The receiver was in need and saw the gift as a means for meeting part but not all of the need and immediately used the funds to reduce the need for food, shelter, clothing, gas to get to work, or utility bills to restore lights, heat, or air conditioning or just a fan. But the underlining problem remained. Meanwhile, the giver, was blessed to have these needs covered by resources with "more than enough" and had the joy of sharing. "A blessing shared is twice as nice, and a burden shared is half as heavy." Yet half the burden remain on the receiver while the giver has twice the blessing that produced the sharing. At times there is a better way: give a man a fish and he will be hungry tomorrow; teach him how to fish and he can happily provide for himself. Givers who have more than enough and can share should not neglect the other part. The giver should share wisdom or know how to enable the receiver to meet the other half of the burden. Remember, the manna God provided the Hebrews on their journey from Egypt to the Promised Land, if more than enough for daily bread were gathered, it spoiled except when saved for the Sabbath.

The Hebrew's Daily Bread.

There were lessons to learn from the Hebrews Daily Bread from God's bounty. It appears God was teaching lessons about planning, working, gathering, and saving in relation to the worship on the Sabbath. The day before the Sabbath was the only day Hebrews could gather "more than enough" and that "overage" was to be used in association with the worship of God. God's manna taught the gathers that when they had more than enough, it would spoil. God even created a Heavenly Treasure Pot, (where manna would not spoil) They were to store manna as evidence to future generations that God's provision was adequate for the Hebrew Nation on their journey. It is important to remember that this provision stopped when they settled on the borders of Canaan. Now, they were back to the Official Edict of God in the Garden: "daily bread is earned by the sweat of your brow." However, forty years of God's supply had taught a special lesson: when you have "more than enough" it is only for kingdom endeavors. If you store it, the extra will spoil. Luke explains where most people store their heart…and it is not in a faith-based facility. The converse of the statement is true. *"Where your **heart** is there your **treasure** will be also."*

> *32. Fear not, little flock; for it is your Father's good pleasure to give you the kingdom. 33. Keep your assets liquid and give alms; provide yourselves a purse that does not grow old, a treasure in the*

heavens that fails not, where no thief has access, neither moths can spoil. 34. For where your treasure is, there your heart will be also. (Luke 12:32-34 EDNT)

Divine Assistance is Available

The over programming in religious groups usually comes from a committee or individual developing a program and then "Praying for God to bless their work." Much of these extra programs are about raising the budget and offerings for special programs. God blesses His Word not necessarily the work of a committee. First, we should pray for spiritual guidance as we study the Word of God to learn about God's plans: then proceed. ***"For I know the plans I have concerning you, declares YAHWEH, 'plans for prosperity and not for harm, to give to you a future and a hope."*** (Jeremiah 29:11 EDOT) This can never happen when the institution plans and schedules all programs and religious endeavors based on materialistic and secular funding.

Go the Second Mile

The lesson of the "second mile" is a good one to learn (Matthew 5:41). A Roman soldier could require a stranger to carry his load for one mile, but no more. Jesus told His followers, *"If one compels you to carry his load one mile, carry the load two."* The first mile was out of duty; the second was obedience to the words of Jesus. The first mile may serve a purpose as an act of obedience, but the second mile becomes a witness and an open door for discussion as to the character of the load-carrier and the attitude toward the task. I am confident that some singled out to carry a Roman soldier's load, must have resented the task. When the words of Jesus were recalled, the attitude and the environment changed for the better. Constructive discipline has its positive reward.

> *11. At the time all discipline is painful rather than pleasant; but afterwards, when it has done the work of discipline, it yields a harvest of good fruit in a righteous life for those trained by the experience.* (Hebrews 12:11 EDNT)

> *14. Remind them of these things, solemnly witnessing before God not to fight with words, for they are not useful but bring destruction to the ones hearing. **15. Be eager to present yourself approved to God, a workman unashamed, cutting straight the word of truth.** 16. But avoid blasphemous and worthless chatter: for they will cause more disobeying of the word. **19. However, the foundation of God stands firm, having this seal, the Lord knows those who are His. And Let everyone who names the name of the Lord stand clear from unrighteousness.*** (2 Timothy 2:14-16,19 EDNT)

Money is about the Future

Money is a link to the past and a bridge to the future. It is linked to past wages, savings, unearned income from investments, and inheritance. Some may see Social Security and retirement income as gifts from the government or a company; however, it is based on years of service, age, and at times on personal health. These funds are not gifts; they were earned over the years and are payment for past labor and services. Money being a bridge to the future is harder for some to understand. The future is either

one of pressing debt or a planned life of service
and a healthy retirement based on wise planning for
many years. Money matters are an important part of
everyone's life and future. The absence of money
speaks loudly, but money in hand whispers family
security and opens doors of opportunity to serve
others and advance the kingdom.

Green and Brown Money

Recently earned money is considered "green"
while money in the bank, unearned income, gifts,
and savings are "brown" money. The more sweat
equity in funds, the greener it becomes. A paycheck
on Friday is wages for work all week and is green
money. Sweat equity adds value to wages, but the
use of brown money is painless spending. Sweat
equity causes more caution in spending green money.
Usually tithes and/or offerings given at a place of
worship comes from green money; therefore, it is
often given reluctantly from a human perspective.
Provided it is a willing gift from a spiritual heart there
is gladness to be able to share; when sweat equity
gets involved there is often a reluctance to part
with money that could be used elsewhere. Brown
money, savings, money in the bank, old money,
and inheritance is without "sweat equity" and the
attachment is less. Tithe and general offerings
come from green money while special gifts may
come from the overage which is normally brown
money. Understanding green and brown money
will assist with placing funds in God's basket for the
advancement of kingdom issues.

Everything is About the Future

Financial transaction must be weighed with reference to the assurance of future income and unexpected expenses. Reckless spending or sharing is not a spiritual virtue. Saint Paul in Ephesians 5:5 was somewhat troubled over wasteful spendthrifts. A purchase is not about the present; it always relates to the future. Should the money be used for some required need? Is income stable enough to replace the money without the risk of loss? Is the purchase absolutely necessary or only an enhanced want? Is there sufficient cash flow to guarantee this purchase? Does it use funds that will be required for other obligations? Are there pressing future obligations that will be hindered by this purchase? Everyone must have a contingency plan relative to money. In the case of a Bank Account, an overdraw privilege, is for an emergency not a regular occurrence. It is expensive to use the banks money to cover a failure to plan ahead. It is best to buy what is needed and save for things that are wanted.

Loans are Debts

It would be good to remember that banks only loan money to those they believe can repay in a timely manner. Then there are predatory lending individuals and/or institutions guilty of "usury" *the illegal practice of lending money at unreasonable rates of interest.* These are more interested in the default possibility than retiring of the loan. The buyer must remember the item being purchased is collateral for the loan and will be lost if the loan is not repaid in a timely manner. ***The rich have power over the borrower and the poor are debtors to the lender.*** (Proverbs 22:7 EDOT)

Necessary Planning

The planning for shortfalls or emergencies include establishing a family savings account with sufficient funds to operate three (3) months without expected income. One cannot spend anticipated funds or live long on credit. This complicates the future and risks permanent loss. Most have financial shortfalls, unexpected emergencies, or expenses. Advance planning is necessary to avert damage and loss.

> *20. This is what Hezekiah did throughout Judah, doing what was good and right and faithful before the* LORD *his God. 21. In everything that he undertook in the service of God's temple and in obedience to the law and the commands,* ***he sought his God and worked whole-heartedly. And so, he prospered.*** (2 Chronicles 31:20-21)

Emergency Family Savings Account

It would be good if each family anticipated three months of expenses and made a special savings account as a contingency fund for a shortfall eventuality. Always plan for these seven (7) areas of ongoing expenses:

1. Average tithe/offerings

2. Food and medicine

3. Mortgage or rent

4. Utilities and repairs

5. Car expenses and required trips

6. Insurance and taxes

7. Entertainment and recreation

There is clear scriptural procedure for advance planning for kingdom projects. Take note of Paul's reminder sent to the Corinthian congregation.

*1.Now concerning the gathering of **funds for the saints**, follow the directions I gave to the congregations of Galatia. 2. On the first day of each week remember how God has prospered you and put aside your gifts in a safe place, so no collections will be necessary when I come. 3. When I arrive whomever you approved by letters, I will send with your freewill gifts to Jerusalem. 4. And if it is advantageous that I go, they shall go with me. 5. I plan to pass through Macedonia and I will visit you when I do. 6. And it may be that I will remain with you through the winter, that you may assist me on the next phase of my journey.* (1 Corinthians 16:1-12 EDNT)

An Understanding Heart

According to my friend Zodhiates, in Psalm 8:1-9:6, wisdom is personified and speaks both simply and profoundly asking the hearer to have an understanding heart. In high places, by the fork of the road, and at the gate of the city, wisdom seeks listeners. Would it not be wise to pay attention to wise words and common sense? In Psalm 8:18-21 below, wisdom speaks of riches, honor, prosperity and wealth... that wisdom is better than gold and surpasses the value of silver. The impact of listening and gaining wisdom would be a rich inheritance that would produce a full treasury.

> *18. With me are riches and honor, with enduring prosperity and wealth. 19. <u>My bounty is better than gold; my increase surpasses refined silver. 20. My footsteps are in honesty and virtue, along the pathway of justice</u>, 21.* **A rich inheritance is bestowed on true followers and their treasuries are made full.** (Proverbs 8:18-21 EDOT)

"When your outgo is more than your income; your upkeep is your downfall."

—A.L.P. GREEN

II

Accessing
The Children's Bread

Mission Priority

Jesus encountered a Gentile woman and initially refused to heal her daughter by saying, *"It is not right to take the children's bread and toss it to the puppies."* Taken out of context, and translated into English, it is easy to mistake this for a racial slur or an insult. But according to both the context and language involved, Jesus was not referring to the woman as a "dog," either directly or indirectly. He was making a point about the priorities He was given for His mission *(to go to the Jews first)*. He was also testing the faith of the woman and teaching an important lesson to His disciples. He applied an idiom to a situation in an effort to explain the priorities of His ministry, and to teach a valuable lesson to His disciples.

Mission Delegation

In Matthew 15, Jesus shared, *"I am not sent but to the lost sheep of the house of Israel."* There are first things, priorities in all situations. In Mark the answer *"Let the children first be filled."* Jesus later shared with his Disciple in John's Gospel "*As the Father has sent Me, even so send I you.* (John 20:21) Jesus was delegating His mission to His followers, trusting they understood the priorities. It was later clear to Paul when he told the Romans, *"For I am never reluctant to preach the gospel: for it is the power of God unto salvation to all who believe; **to the Jew first, and also to the Greek.**"* (Romans 1:16)

> *27. But Jesus said to her, Let the children first be satisfied: for it is not right to take the **children's bread,** and to throw it to the house-puppies. 28. And she answered, Yes, Lord: yet the puppies under the table eat of the **children's crumbs**. 29. And He said to her, For this saying, go your way; the evil spirit has left your daughter.* (Mark 7:24-30 EDNT)

Gentile Territory

In those days Jews often referred to non-Jews as "dogs." In Greek, this word is *kuon*, meaning "cur" or a nameless, mixed-breed dog. (Matthew 7:6; Luke 16:21; Philippians 3:2). Non-Jews were considered so unspiritual that even being in their presence could make a Jew ceremonially unclean (John 18:28). Much of Jesus' ministry, however, involved turning expectations and prejudices around in favor of the offended (Matthew 11:19; John 4:9–10). According to Matthew's narrative, Jesus left Israel and went into Tyre and Sidon, which was Gentile territory (Matthew 15:21). When the Canaanite woman approached and repeatedly asked for healing, the disciples were annoyed and asked Jesus to send her away (Matthew 15:23).

At this point, Jesus explained the priority of His current ministry in a way that both the woman and the disciples could understand. Presently, His duty was to the people of Israel, not to the Gentiles (Matthew 15:24). It would be reckless for Jesus to take His attention from Israel, in violation of His mission. It would be similar to a father taking food from his children in order to throw it to their pets under the table. (Matthews 15:26) The exact word Jesus used, in the Greek, was *kunarion*, meaning "little dog" or "puppies" (a child's pet), He did not use *kuon,* meaning "cur" or was He referring to unspiritual people or to an "unclean" animal. It is easy for some to criticize something they do not understand.

Great Faith Granted Request

Jesus frequently tested people to evaluate their intentions, often through response questions or challenges (see John 4:16–18; and 4:50–53). His response to the Canaanite woman is similar. In testing her, Jesus declined her request and explained that she had no legitimate expectation of His assistance. The woman, however, lived out the principle Jesus Himself taught in the parable of the persistent widow (Luke 18:1–8). Her response proved that she understood fully what Jesus was saying, yet had enough conviction to ask anyway (Matthew 15:27). Jesus acknowledged her faith—calling it "great"—and granted her request for the healing of her daughter.

Not by Bread Alone

Born-again believers who walk in fellowship with Jesus have access to the **Children's Bread**. Jesus taught His followers to pray for work to earn their daily bread. He was not asking them to pray for a hand out. Daily bread is defined *"as money or food needed in order to live."* Current dictionaries define "bread" as *dough, cash, finance, currency, bucks, food, sustenance, or nourishment.* The word *bread* has become a substitute or colloquial expression for "money" for many generations. Scripture is clear, Jesus is quoting Deuteronomy 8:2-3: *"Man shall not live by bread alone...but by every word that proceeds from the mouth of God?"* (Matthew 4:4; Luke 4:4) The first recorded words of Jesus after beginning His ministry was to assert the authority of scripture, *"It is written"* and He was addressing Satan *"Man shall not live by bread alone, but by every word that proceeds out of the mouth of God."* On this occasion Jesus was referring to stones that looked like bread. The word used means "thing" or a clear understanding would be "anything that looks like bread (or money earned by work and sweat): but by the living Word from the Divine Source. The point was that man should accept everything that God ordains over and above the work of his own hands. (Genesis 3:19)

> *16 He gave you manna to eat in the wilderness, something your ancestors had never known, to humble and test you so that in the end it might go well with you. 17 You may say to yourself, "My power and the strength of my hands have produced this wealth for me."* **18 But remember the LORD your God, for it is he who gives you the ability to produce wealth, and so confirms his covenant, which he swore to your ancestors, as it is today.** (Deuteronomy 8:16-18 NIV)

A Gift of God

18 This is what I have observed to be good: that it is appropriate for a person to eat, to drink and to find **satisfaction in their toilsome labor** *under the sun during the few days of life God has given them— for this is their lot.* *19* Moreover, **when God gives someone wealth and possessions, and the ability to enjoy them, to accept their lot and be happy in their toil**—*this is a gift of God.* *20* They seldom reflect on the days of their life, because God keeps them occupied with gladness of heart. (Ecclesiastes 5:18-20 NIV)

Profit at the Farmer's Market

Mother was a widow with three children. She gave up her teaching job because being paid 8 and 1/2 months a year she was unable to provide for her family during the summer. She took a job in a textile mill for $6 to $8 a week on piece work. Being a male child with two sisters, I began working at age 10, doing what I could to assist. By the time I was fourteen, an uncle, Hiram Green, was letting me work during the summer of 1943 at the Farmer's Market in Chattanooga selling his farm produce. Hiram would continually restock with fresh products. This required me to stay overnight and sleep in the truck.   He would let me eat out of his money, and the freedom, trust, and a taste of independence was refreshing. Most able-bodied people prefer work to charity. And with no air conditioning in those days there was a lot of summer sweat (according to God's agreement with

Adam). At least, that is how mother explained hard work to me.

Hard Work Means Extra Income

Realizing that many of the farmers wanted to go home at night, I watched the market about closing time looking for farmers with unsold produce who wanted to go home. Since I had to stay overnight anyway, I would use my uncle's money and buy their produce at a bargain, so they could go home. Selling their produce, the next morning at a good profit, I would put my uncle's money back and pocket the profit. Some weeks I would make more money than my mother by this extra work. It was a time of growing and understanding how things worked. At the end of the summer, my uncle would give me a small stipend, reminding me he had fed me all summer, and I would thank him. It was years before he knew that I had used his money to make a profit for myself. Naturally, mother thought my uncle had paid me well.

Business Lessons Learned

The lessons learned included that *"all work is God's business"* designed to provide funds for family needs, faith-based offerings, and future plans. Yes, mother taught me to tithe! It was also good to learn that a little initiative could improve your circumstance in life and that one must take advantage of each opportunity to work hard and earn an honest dollar. The money was a great boost to the family income and provided for my clothes, school supplies, and a little pocket money for a poor boy. Later, I learned that most businessmen use a bank loan to buy their products, and then paid back the loan (with interest) when the product was sold. My arrangement was better because I used Hiram's money without interest. Everybody won: Hiram got a cheap worker to stay 24/7 at the Farmer's Market and sell his produce, and I made an extra profit from buying and selling. It was a time of learning; one lesson was clear: ***"Friends are better than money in the bank because you can use the interest without reducing the principle."*** When those friends are **family**; it is even better. The extra money was a great assistance to the family's meager budget, too.

Traveling the Right Path

It is better to stumble along the Right Path than run down the wrong road. According to my son, Barton, *"A stumble requires a quick step to keep from falling."* The Scriptural definition of stumble is *"cause to sin."* Joseph is a good example of a young man who stayed on the path chosen for him by Providence. Yes, he was a common worker, but God was with him and he soon advanced to an important position. Sure, there were dangerous and treacherous patches on the journey, but God had pointed him in the right direction to obtain the purpose God had determined for his life. Even when betrayed by family and friends, he was in the Hands of God. Joseph learned that staying on the Right Path is part of God's plan to handle the big problems of life.

2. I will go before you and will level the mountains; I will break down gates of bronze and cut through bars

*of iron. 3.**I will give you hidden treasures, riches stored in secret places, so that you may know that I am the LORD,** the God, who summons you by name.* (Isaiah 45:2-3 NIV)

Stay the Course

Sibling jealousy brought trouble for Joseph's life, but God had a good plan for him. He became a trusted assistant to Pharaoh and the jealous and evil plan turned into good and the lives of many were saved, even those who had mistreated him. Often the young are troubled when God's plan is not clearly understood. The rule is to stay the course and live a clean and moral life and the end of life will be better than the beginning. Joseph was not in Egypt by choice, but God had an unknown plan that was not understood by others. Mistreated by his brothers, Joseph ended as a slave laborer in a strange land with a grieving father left behind. But it was the right path for him and the future needs of his family. As a strong young Hebrew man, Joseph was tempted by Potiphar's wife, but he stayed the course and continued to follow the right path of basic morality and ethics. On this path God led him to save his family and many others including the brothers who sold him into slavery.

Now Joseph had been taken down to Egypt. Potiphar, an Egyptian who was one of Pharaoh's officials, the captain of the guard, bought him from the Ishmaelites who had taken him there. 2 The LORD was with Joseph so that he prospered, and he lived in the house of his Egyptian master. 3 When his master saw that the LORD was with him and that the LORD gave him success in everything he did, *4* Joseph found favor in his eyes and became his attendant. Potiphar put him in charge of his household, and he entrusted to his care everything he owned. *5* From the time he put him in charge of his *household and of all that he owned, the LORD blessed the household of the Egyptian because of Joseph. The blessing of the LORD was on everything Potiphar had, both in the house and in the field.* *6* So Potiphar left everything he had in Joseph's care; with Joseph in charge, he did not concern himself with anything except the food he ate. **Now Joseph was well-built and handsome, *7*** and after a while his master's wife took notice of Joseph and said, "Come to bed with me!" *8* But he refused. "With me in charge," he told her, "my master does not concern himself with anything in the house; everything he owns he has entrusted to my care. *9* No one is greater in this house than I am. My master has withheld nothing from me except you, because you are his wife. How then could I do such a wicked thing and sin against God?" *10* And though she spoke to Joseph day after day, he refused to go to bed with her or even be with her. *11* One day he went into the house to attend to his duties, and none of the household servants were inside. *12* She caught him by his cloak and said, "Come to bed with me!" But he left his cloak in her hand and ran out of the house. {Genesis 39-40 NIV)

Keep your Fork

A Pastor visiting a dying man to discuss particulars of his final service. He had only one request, ***"Bury me with a fork in my hand."*** The pastor did not clearly understand, the man explained; *"In some eating places the waiter will ask that you*

keep your fork for dessert. I want a fork in my hand
because something good is ahead for me in heaven."
Understanding the function of a fork is liberating: it
is an implement used to lift food to the mouth, hold a
steak while cutting, or for keeping for the sweet things
that are coming. **Not a bad idea:** we should all keep
a positive attitude about the future and that the end of
life is what the first of life was about. When you have
and understand about the fork, you are ready for the
future.... whatever comes down the path.

> *7* One person pretends to be rich, yet has nothing;
> another pre-tends to be poor, yet has great wealth.
> *8* A person's riches may ransom their life, but the
> poor cannot respond to threatening rebukes. *9* The
> light of the righteous shines brightly, but the lamp of
> the wicked is snuffed out. *10* Where there is strife,
> there is pride, but wisdom is found in those who take
> advice. *11* Dishonest money dwindles away, but
> whoever gathers money little by little makes it grow.
> (Proverbs 13:7-11 NIV)

Institutionalized vs Personalized Weapons

Most Faith-based groups depend on
institutionalized plans; such as, fund-raising
Campaigns, Kick-off events, and a multitude of
other gimmicks to support their local budget and
missionary projects. These promotions, although
they work among those with a secular mindset, are
an admission that Faith-based groups do not clearly
understand Kingdom economics or the multiple
segments of personal wealth; such as, work to
support the needs of family, income over and above
this need are to assist the poor, and **"more than**

enough" to share with kingdom enterprises. *"Where God guides He provide"* may be a worthy saying, but it does not eliminate hard work or good budget planning.

> *27. And whoever does not bear his own cross and follow Me, cannot be My disciple. 28. For which of you,* **intending to build a lofty structure do not first estimate the cost to see if there are sufficient funds to complete the project? 29. Lest after you have made the foundation you are unable to finish it,** *all those watching begin to ridicule him. 30. Saying, This man began to build and was unable to finish.* (Luke 14:27-30 EDNT)

There is clear scriptural procedure for advance planning for kingdom projects. Take note of Paul's reminder sent to the Corinthian congregation.

> *1.Now concerning the gathering of* **funds for the saints,** *follow the directions I gave to the congregations of Galatia. 2. On the first day of each week remember how God has prospered you and put aside your gifts in a safe place, so no collections will be necessary when I come. 3. When I arrive whomever you approved by letters, I will send with your freewill gifts to Jerusalem. 4. And if it is advantageous that I go, they shall go with me. 5. I plan to pass through Macedonia and I will visit you when I do. 6. And it may be that I will remain with you through the winter, that you may assist me on the next phase of my journey.* (1 Corinthians 16:1-12 EDNT)

The Proven Pathway

The proven pathway to adequate finance for the family and God's work is to do it God's way: tithes and offerings on a regular basis and a plan to share "overage" in personal income and accumulated wealth after the needs and obligations of family are met. Although the Word teaches to *"seek first the kingdom of God and His righteous equity, and all these things will be added to you,"* it was prefaced by Jesus' words about food, drink, and clothes, ***"Your heavenly Father knows that you need all these things."*** The Word also, places a primary responsibility on support for the family as a mark of spiritual commitment. ***If anyone provides not for his own people, and especially his family, he has denied the faith, and is (untrustworthy) and worse than an unbeliever.*** (1 Timothy 5:8 EDNT)

Tools must fit the User

David in scripture could not use the institutionalized weapons; instead he used his familiar sling and a smooth pebble to defeat the giant that terrorized Israel's army. David took the facts of Israel's desperate situation and disassembled the weapons of warfare that would not work for him and used initiative and familiar tools together with the guiding hand of God to win the battle against the giant. The shepherd lad could not fight Goliath in the sophisticated armor of King Saul. The weapons of the monarch were not suitable for this poor shepherd boy's personal use. Tools must fit the hand of the user to insure a good outcome. David also anticipated the next step and selected five stones because Goliath had four brothers. **Now that was good budget planning in the stone age**. David not only used personal initiative and refused to use tools structured by others. A small stone and a handmade slingshot with God's assistance won the battle. All workers must be willing participants in the process using **familiar** tools they readily understand how to use.

Good Family Men Selected to Lead

After the selection of seven good men to assist the Apostles with the needs of widows, one of the seven, Steven was arrested and presented a scorcher of a sermon about promises to Abraham, the life of Joseph in Egypt, Moses, the burning bush, and all about Israel's deliverance from bondage, the Red Sea experience, the Ten Commandments and the wilderness story of how Moses was resisted by the people who turned their hearts away from God and looked back toward Egypt. They stoned Stephen and persecution broke out against the believers in Jerusalem and the Greek speaking saints were scattered.

Good Men Able to Influence Others

Saul of Tarsus had consented to the death of Stephen and began to cause chaos among the Greek speaking saints. Somehow, he understood that these converts were good men and would be able to influence other Jews to follow Jesus. Thus, the harassment and suffering drove them out of the city into the Greek speaking world. *As a result, those who were scattered in different directions went from place to place declaring the gospel.* (Acts 8:4 EDNT) When these good men were pushed out of their comfort zone in Jerusalem by persecution, they began to evangelize *"as they traveled"* and the gospel was greatly advanced.   Often an evil strategy against the gospel backfires and the kingdom is advanced. Similar to Joseph where his brothers meant their action as evil; God had a good purpose for Joseph being in Egypt. It is clear that good stable converts become an asset to moral and ethical matters whenever and wherever they go. They automatically *"do as they go"* according to the Believers Challenge by Jesus "**as you go make disciples.**" (Matthew 28:19 EDNT) This has been the case throughout recorded human history.

A Spiritual Journey

An official from Ethiopia seeking a closer relationship with God traveled to Jerusalem to worship and search for ways to improve his spiritual journey. As a Gentile, he did not have access to the table in the place of worship but was able to secure a copy of the scroll of Isaiah as a source of spiritual enrichment. The book of Isaiah was exactly what he needed, a fresh message about the Messiah and a good read for a Gentile seeking a deeper life.   Reading this scroll as he journeyed, the Ethiopian became part of a spiritual experience that changed the outreach mindset of the early believers in Jerusalem. Philip joined the Ethiopian in the chariot, *the eunuch said to Philip, Tell me about whom the prophet is speaking of Himself or of another? Then Philip began at the same verse and shared the good news about Jesus. As they traveled on, they came to some water: and the eunuch said, What hinders me from being baptized*? (Acts 8:34-36 EDNT) The sincere seeker who was denied access to the Temple was initiated into the kingdom of God and given a seat at the Lord's Table.

A Walk in the Desert

Ethiopia is one of the oldest independent country in Africa, and the Christian church there owes its existence to the spiritual hunger of a seeking man and the obedience of deacon Philip, who was led by the Spirit to move away from a stable situation and to actively follow the Spirit for a walk in the desert. God prepared the saint, created desire in the heart of a sinner, provided the written word, and gave Philip an opportunity to explain about Jesus. The expansion of the kingdom comes from the obedience of saints and the need of seekers.

The Path less Traveled

All believers should clearly understand that the force that brought the Ethiopian into the kingdom remains at work; it was not the assembled congregation in Jerusalem that reached this man, but the obedient walk of a believer who took the Gospel to one seeking to understand. Obedience to the guidance of the Spirit will cause a believer to take the right path at the right time. It appears that God alone adequately prepares the seeker for conversion, a saint for straightforward witnessing, creates the situational encounter between saint and seeker, provides useable material and opens the door for sharing the good news of saving grace. Perhaps more believers should take a walk on the road less traveled and be available as a witness to those seeking a connection with God and a better way of life.

God's Adverbs

(An excerpt from Green, Hollis L. SO TALES, (2011). Global. Nashville)

Traveling alone down Interstate 75 south of Atlanta, the long journey ahead suggested a hitch hiker might be good company. As the young man entered the car, ***"Good morning, my name is Hollis Green; I am a Christian."*** The response *was "**Carl Krudof, I am a philosopher."*** The young philosopher was baited, "Do you write your philosophy down, or do you just talk?" He claimed to write important thoughts down. He was asked about his most recent writings. Carl said, "I have just written a definition of God, but I don't believe there is one." [A definition of God by a philosopher who doesn't believe in God. This was going to be interesting.]

Reaching into the back seat to retrieve a small unzipped notebook, Carl began to read: "God is the singular, possessive, abstraction of the adverb."

[He is a philosopher; my teachers talked that way. Carl was asked to repeat the first statement.]

He repeated, "God is the singular, possessive, abstraction of the adverb."

[What's an adverb? I've been out of school too long.]

Carl continued, *"An adverb is the linguistic manifestation of a life process."*

It is my conviction that God prepares both the saint and the seeker and provides the situation and the supplies to share with others the good news. The discussion centered on Carl's definition of God. It was good theology for a philosopher who did not believe in God. This was discussed at length. His use of the **present tense** initiated a long exchange. The **singularity of one God** was discussed. The **possessive nature of God** was considered. God's ways being past finding out are kind of an **abstraction**. Somewhere in Carl's intellectual comprehension, the use and function of the adverb was the key to an adequate perception of God.

He continued to read *"An adverb is the linguistic manifestation of a life process."* God was not viable in Carl's life because there was no systematic order relating the signs and symbols about a Divine Person to his personal reality. God in this case was the big Noun, and Carl had never witnessed the action of God in real time. He needed someone who had personally experienced the present tense power and action of God to adjust the semantics and syntax of the experience to a language he could accept. Carl needed the same touch of experiential reality that Thomas of scripture desired. Carl needed a personal touch of the hand of faith. He needed to see a manifestation of the resurrected life of Jesus. At last, the course of action was clear. Carl needed to see one of God's adverbs.

This called for a new introduction, *"**Good morning, my name is Hollis Green; I am one of God's adverbs.**"* A spark of cognition was ignited; Carl's mind was open; the heart was ready; and the Holy Spirit had done His work. A simple walk down the Roman Road of scripture brought Carl face to face with the reality of the God who became man whose name was Jesus. He accepted not only the present tense existence of the Creator, but a personal relationship with Jesus, the Son, the Spirit had cut through the academic mind of Carl and he was changed from a doubting stranger into a believing Brother. He was greeted as a fellow adverb and took his first steps on the Right Path to fellowship with the real-time action of God. He was encouraged to find other believers with whom to fellowship where he could develop a missional reality.

III

Living
A Missional Reality

More of God's Adverbs are Needed

What the world needs is more of God's Adverbs sharing the excitement of living the Christian life. Are you willing to be one of God's Adverbs ready to magnify and point to the blessings of God that are available to all who believe? If so, blessings are on the way. It is always a joy to share the testimony of grace with someone who is reaching for divine assistance. This is living a missional realty.

Missional Living

Wisdom brings authenticity and genuineness to the daily lives of those desiring a missional lifestyle. In Christianity, **missional living is the adoption of the attitude, thinking, behaviors, and practices of a missionary in order to engage others in the process of advancing the gospel message**. In Psalm 8: 32-35 wisdom speaks further to the faithful who attend with interest to instruction and are blessed by keeping to the proper pathway. There is a warning not to disregard the lessons learned. Those who listen and are watchful daily at the open door of wisdom will find life and favor from the Lord and will enjoy a missional reality. This is the day for fellowship among the band of believers; time to freely access the children's bread.

> 1. *As we work together with God, we appeal to you not to accept the grace of God and let it go to waste.* 2. *God said, I have heard your prayers at a convenient time, and in the day of salvation I have brought you relief in a difficult situation: **observe, now is the time for coming together; now is the day of deliverance.*** (2 Corinthians 6:1-2 EDNT)

Rediscovering the True Identity

The *missional* construct rediscovers the true identity of *"those belonging to the Lord"* as spiritual witnesses to the world and understands the final words of Jesus to His followers, as a Lifestyle Challenge to Believers rather than a program for an organized house of worship. In the scripture below please notice that Jesus was speaking directly to His followers about **His authority and power** and **sharing what He expected in their future behavior,** *"as you go make disciples of all nations"* reminding **them to identify future disciples with the work of the Godhead**: the Father is the Forgiver; the Son is the Savior; the Holy Spirit is the Comforter, Enlightener, and *Paraclete* (called to assist and encourage) enabling believers to daily walk the missional pathway of unselfish service and realize that the end of the journey is worth the spiritual lifestyle.

Moving beyond Structured Programs

The construct of missional in this book moves beyond the programs of structured Faith-based operations, organized local assemblies, and Christian gatherings. Missional does not see the gathering "places" for worship as primarily an organized activity, but rather the individual's response to the worth-ship of God in the act of personal worship. A missional reality goes beyond the pursuit of churchgoing and the reaching of converts in the process of individual involvement in "disciple making" and funding the global Kingdom advance.

A "value-added" Asset

Salvation and growth in grace and knowledge are a "value added" asset to enable believers to participate in a global outreach and understand how Kingdom economics and personal wealth contribute to the stability of the family and the support and operation of personalized ministries. A missional mindset should produce in believers the attributes and attitudes that demonstrate their ability and predisposition in a lifestyle that is recognized by the community. Witnessing is literally "lifestyle behavior" in contrast to that of non-believers and is the tried and true method of advancing the Kingdom of God.

A Lifestyle Reality

This is a reality that supports a lifestyle! Essentially, a missional reality coalesces around a personalized spirituality that offers a theological shift, a sociological recognition, and a distinct lifestyle for believers. The missional mindset is placed in the context of viewing the Cross through the Empty Tomb, seeing culture as a vehicle of communication, understanding the church as a force with which to work, and the community with the regions beyond as a mission field ready for harvest.

A Pristine view of Missional Lifestyle

*22. You must be honest with yourselves and live by the word not merely hear it. 23. But those who listens to the word, and do not behave it, are similar to a man seeing his own face in a mirror; 24. he observes his flaws, and immediately forgets the man he saw. 25. But whosoever bows down to observe the complete prescriptive usage and the unrestrained opportunity to continue in the word and not become a forgetful hearer, but one who behaves the prescribed deeds, this man shall by the blood be set apart for consecrated action. 26. **If any man among you seem to be devout, and restrains not his unnatural language, he deceives his own heart and his service to God is ineffective.** (James 1:19-26 EDNT)*

An Unadulterated Missional Leader

27. Free from all that would dim the transparency in belief and conduct before God and the Father is this, to go see and relieve the orphans without a father's protection and the women lacking a husband in their distress, and to keep himself untainted by the world. (James 1 :27 EDNT)

A Self-defeating Theology

A change in the KJV translation that made a difference were the words in Matthew (28:19, 20) *19. Go ye therefore, and teach all nations, baptizing them in the name of the Father, and of the Son, and of the Holy Ghost: 20. Teaching them to observe all things whatsoever I have commanded you: and, lo, I am with you always, even unto the end of the world. Amen.* (KJV) This rendering of Jesus' words became a self-defeating theology.

A Fresh Consideration

A fresh consideration for the primary command of the verse translated "teach" would provide a clear understanding: the Greek word used was *matheteuo, to instruct with the purpose of making a disciple; the word suggested not only to learn but to be attached to and become a follower of the teacher.* Greek words have special designations, *matheteuo* here was classified as *aorist imperative active* which denotes a command, or entreaty and indicates the action as being accomplished by the subject of the verb. Later versions translated the word as "make disciples" which was better. Yet, in most translations the *participle* "going" remains an *imperative* "go." This makes the words of Jesus a theology of coercion in an effort to compel followers to "go and do" instead of a missional lifestyle "doing as they go." This was not a Commission for the Church, but more accurately a plan of action for all believers as they daily traveled. This was a Believers Challenge to a ministry of disciple making. They were to make converts as they spread the Gospel by the process of creating learners who through the "disciple making" process of conversion, the sacrament of Identification with the Godhead, and equipping converts with all the known instructions of Jesus. The scriptures below make the intention of Jesus clear:

The Challenge of Jesus

The main problem with the translation of Jesus' Challenge is that it was not given as a Commission to an established or organized assembly, but clear instructions given to the close followers of Jesus as guidance for their spiritual journey. Another basic problem relates to the three participles: Go [*going* or *as you go*] ... *baptizing* ... *teaching* --each participles dependent upon the main verb *teach* translated "make disciples." Although such a verbal construction was not uncommon for the participles themselves to assume the force of a weak imperative, similar to the indirect command in modern English, i.e. "**As you go, close the door**!" However, the command "*make disciples*" is the primary command, while the participles served as weak commands: **going**, **baptizing** and *teaching* are procedures for fulfilling the primary mission clearly stated by the challenge of Jesus. The concept of *"as you go"* was clearly understood by those who heard His words. They also understood they were to wait for the empowerment and confidence-building of the Spirit before beginning the journey.

A Participle is not an Imperative

Some translators render one of three Greek participles, "*going or as you go,*" as an imperative, a direct command. This places a different emphasis on the words of Jesus and creates a strong-arm theology not intended for His volunteer followers. The only direct command (imperative) was *"teach or make disciples"* in the challenge of all four verb forms, *"Go ... make disciples ... baptizing ... teaching"* but early translators chose to make "go" and "teach/make disciples" direct commands, but neglected to use the same rule with *baptizing* and *teaching*. One should either make all the participles into weak commands or leave all the verb form as participles as originally written. Then the instruction of Jesus would harmonize the three participles with the main command and the going, baptizing, and teaching would have common value.   The follow up of going, (baptizing and teaching) are equally as important as the original step on the journey. Why do we emphasize the going and neglect the identification of converts with the full work of the Godhead together with teaching all that Jesus taught early disciples?

What difference does this make?

There are cultural and academic explanations for the above translation which created a self-defeating theology of coercion in an effort to compel people to *"go and do"* rather than establish a *"do as you go"* *missional* lifestyle. Organized leadership consequently spend inordinate energy in the ***"go and do"*** and little effort in dealing **"do as you go"** including baptizing converts and teaching disciples. Converts are to be identified with the full work of the Trinity through baptism and taught to observe instructions that Jesus gave His disciples. This is why converts are baptized in the *"Name (authority) of the Father, the Son, and* *the Holy Spirit"* as foundational identification with the Trinity to start them on the right path of discipleship and developing a missional lifestyle.

Water Baptism Instruction is Incomplete

When water baptism becomes a one-time rite for others to observe without the complete teaching/ learning to be identified with the role of the Trinity in their life, the Candidate has been shortchanged and will demonstrate a weak understanding and value of Holy Communion and other functions designed to keep a believer current in relationship with God; such as, freely giving of themselves, worship participation, using their time, talent, and resources for advancing the kingdom, ongoing fellowship, and outreach efforts for the cure of souls.   Since Water Baptism and Holy Communion are two significant sacraments instituted by Jesus, Candidates are not prepared to take on a mature missional lifestyle and true worship with full involvement of the Trinity in their life and worship without early exposure to spiritual guidance in these areas.

A Challenge to Action

What some call the Great Commission was not a command to "go," but a challenge to action for people already in the process of going into the known world to carry the good news. They were instructed by Jesus to wait for the power of the Spirit. It was guidance to effectively follow-up those who received the teaching, embraced the teacher, and became an active learner. Why would scholars make such a decision that changed the meaning of the words of Jesus? All academics and theologians are influence by an intellectual and cultural bias that takes years and firm methodology to control.

Academic and Cultural Bias

In the England of 1604-1611, the concept of building an Empire was just beginning. To build a British Empire required Englishmen to leave their island fortress and colonize the new world. The Court of Queen Elizabeth and the golden age of English art, literature, and adventure were precursors to this effort. It was 1585 when the first effort to export the golden age was made "to go across the sea" and settle the new land "Virginia," named after the virgin Queen. Although this group nearly starved before Sir Frances Drake rescued the survivors, yet the concept of "go and do" was established in the minds of English achievers.   Consequently, the translators seeking to please the new king, James, used an obscure Greek rule to translate a participle as an imperative: "*Go into all the world…*" This created a program of pressure that caused an artificial incentive that negated the power of the Spirit and personal experience -- which are the true means of advancing Christianity. This was a Challenge of Jesus to support a missional lifestyle of making disciples *"as you go"* rather than a program of *"go and do."* The verses below make clear the intention of Jesus:

> *14. Afterward He appeared to the eleven as they were eating, and reproved for their lack of faith and stubbornness, because they did not believe those who*

had seen Him after He stood up from the grave. 15. And He said, **As you journey to the whole world, proclaim a good message to every inhabitant. 16. He who believes and is baptized will be saved;** *but he who believes not will be condemned.* (Mark 16:14-18 EDNT)

45. Then He opened their understanding, that they might grasp the meaning of the scriptures. 46. And said, Scripture clearly says that Messiah should suffer, and stand up from the grave the third day: 47. and **that repentance and forgiveness of sins should be proclaimed in His name among all nations, starting at Jerusalem. 48. And you are witnesses of these things. 49. And, behold, I send the promise of My Father: but you must wait expectantly in the city of Jerusalem, until you be clothed with ability and heavenly strength.** (Luke 24:45-49 EDNT)

19. Then the same day at evening, being the day one of the week, when the doors were shut where the disciples were assembled for fear of the Jews, Jesus came and stood among them, and said, Peace to you. 20. And when He had spoken, He showed them His hands and side. When the disciples saw the Lord, they were glad. 21. **Then Jesus said again, Peace to you: <u>as my Father, has sent Me, even so send I you.</u> 22. And when He said this, He breathed on them, and said, Receive the Holy Spiri**t: (John 20:19-22 EDNT)

6. On one occasion the apostles asked Him, Lord will you now restore the kingdom to Israel? 7. He answered, It is not for you to know the period of time or the specific season, that is only in the Father's authority. 8. **But you shall receive miraculous ability and strength, after the Holy Spirit is come** *upon you: and you shall be My witnesses unto the death both in Jerusalem, and in all Judaea, and in Samaria, and continually into the farthest part of the earth.* (Acts 1:6-8 EDNT)

A Form of Godliness

Gathering in a particular place to be entertained or participate in a form of worship that fails to demonstrate the value of God in all aspects of life is a fraud. A form of godliness in worship without power or lifestyle behavior that is not missional does not acknowledge the *"worth-ship"* of God or prompt the taking of the message of peace, love, and eternal life to the world. It is less than pure religion. Faith-based worship should impact a missional reality in the life of Believers and encourage a positive worldview. The words of James, the forceful leader of a pristine congregation of early believers in Jerusalem are appropriate here:

A Message to Early Believers

19. Wherefore, my cherished band of believers let everyone be swift to hear, slow to speak, slow to wrath: 19. because of the righteousness of God, let everyone be ready listeners, slow to express our mind, slow to take offence: 20. for anger does not bear fruit acceptable to God. 21. **Wherefore put aside all moral corruption and the abundance of worthless behavior and receive with a <u>teachable spirit the firmly established word, which is able to make safe that spiritual part of you that determines all behavior.</u>** (James 1:9-21 EDNT)

A Muddled Message

Western world leadership muddled the message of grace by accepting a watered-down orthodoxy which included variations of sectarian dogma, geographical culture, personal convictions, and social attitudes that predetermine how situations were to be viewed, questions answered, and sacred scripture construed. It appears they understood the Gospel and the benefits of religion "*as a commodity*" available only for habitual churchgoers. Such self-righteous groups are better described as having "*name brand religion*" which uses past history and events as "*freeze-frame theology*" to defend their lack of relevance to the lives of real people and humanity as a whole. This includes the matter of Faith-based economics and personal wealth.

> *1. Know this that dangerous times will come in the last days. 2. For men will be self-lovers, **lovers of money**, arrogant boasters, treating God and sacred things disrespectfully, disobedient to parents, unthankful, wicked, 3. without family affection, true-breakers, false accusers, without sexual restraint, violent, despisers of all that is good, 4. traitors, stubborn, lovers of pleasure more than lovers of God; 5. **having an outward façade of religion, but rejecting the moral instructions and are strangers to the influence of the Spirit:** from such turn away.* (2 Timothy 3:1-5 EDNT

An Unlearned Lesson of History

The world did not learn the lesson that came from the fall of Germany. Germanic leadership was obvious in academics, business, inventions, and in the production of theological textbooks. Yet, their churches failed to influence the behavior of the population. This tragedy was clear in the life and death of Dietrich Bonhoeffer. During the buildup to WWII, Hitler and the Third Reich demonstrated opposition to Judaism, began to control all religions and took measures to bring the German church under Nazi supervision. Bonhoeffer faced death in a Nazi prison because of his personal courage by resisting governmental control of the German church.

Concepts of Principled Responsibility

Through the Confessing Church, Bonhoeffer began to develop his concepts of principled responsibility in relation to the spiritual life and personal resistance to governmental infringement on places of worship. During his imprisonment, he worked further on a lifestyle approach to discipleship. It took real courage to live the disciplined life during the Nazi period, but perhaps it takes more audacity and spiritual courage to resist secularization of the faith-based community in times of peace. Silently, civil government has encroached on the sacredness of marriage, life of the unborn, issues of death and dying, and some matters of conscience that have been the purview of religion for centuries. Only missional behavior and lifestyle can resist this encroachment and this can only be done with the assistance of the Holy Spirit.

An Antecedent Obligation

Although Bonhoeffer made fragmentary suggestions about a time when there would be a "religion-less society," his insights and understanding developed during the cauldron and instability of war should alarm all faith-based people. His statements concerned the reality of Christian faith, not the formal, public expression of religion. He believed that faith-based people had an antecedent obligation that binds them together as a social force to complete certain responsibility. He suggested that the meanness of war annihilated this viable historical possibility for Germany and much of the world. Few know that Bonhoeffer wrote seven (7) theses on "youth work" and his primary mission was to have confessing believers available to lead Germany after the war. In fact, he had a chance to extend his visit to America and remain safe, but his drive to prepare young leaders to salvage the ravages of war caused him to return to Germany and ultimately give his life for the cause.

Ten Good Men could not be Found

Could fifty men with Bonhoeffer's commitment have save Germany and the world the tragedy of war. Finally, Abraham ask God to spare Sodom from destruction if ten (10) righteous men could be found. In Genesis 18 God agreed! Not 50 not even 10 could be found.   One man can do much; a few good men can do more, but God wanted fifth (50) but finally agreed to only ten (10) good men with a life of righteousness before destruction could be avoided.

Where were the ten good men that God requires to bring safety, morality, and security to the city? Little is much when God is in it; evidently Germany did not have even ten (10) men of the character and caliber of Bonhoeffer and Europe and the whole world suffered and still suffer from the lack of a few who will resist the evil in the world required by God to prevent destruction of both the good and bad. What does this say about my town or your city? Perhaps we should stop "playing church" and start truly worshipping the Almighty in Spirit and in Truth!

Faith and the Inhumanity of War

Looking at the tragedy of war, Bonhoeffer understood that German preaching and teaching did not create a human conscience to prevent the inhumanity of armed conflict during the decades of two world wars.   The tragedy of warfare crushed the internal principles by which Germany engaged the world and the wartime atrocities were committed by men who had been under the influence of the German church for decades. The tragedy, according to Bonhoeffer, was that the songs and sermons on Sunday had no influence on the social policies of the government or the personal behavior of the German soldier. Why, because there were no lifestyle witnesses to the saving Grace of God active and visible. There were only a few "spiritual adverbs" who pointed to the authority of God and the truthfulness, honor and reliability embodied in humanity. There were others, but Dietrich Bonhoeffer was alone on the morning of April 9, 1945. Bonhoeffer was only 39 when he was stripped naked and hanged by the Gestapo. Yet his legacy lives and Germany and the world benefited from his life. His legacy still speaks volumes to those who will listen and follow his example of a faith-based lifestyle regardless of the cost of the journey.

A False Witness

To disguise religious activity as spiritual work is deception, sacrilege and a *"false witness"* is on a list of things which God hates. (Proverbs 6:16-19) Camouflage is used to conceal when an adversary does not wish to be recognizable. Some disguise declining local participation in terms of a migrating population or changing communities. The obscuring of decline deceives the public by self-serving explanations; such as, redecorating buildings, adding space, landscaping, putting up new signs, or adding other trappings of progress and unnecessary embellishments to attempt to display prosperity.

Where are the True Saints?

Some small groups claim the membership has settled to a *"despised few"* because of their emphasis on quality rather than quantity. Provided there were ten righteous among the few, God would bless their gatherings. Despite the method of concealment or the change in appurtenances of property, the influence faith-based group once had on the community has weakened or become nonexistent. Weddings, funerals, feeding the poor and other sponsored events have taken on a civil or social identity rather than being seen as a sacramental experience. These self-serving explanations have disguised the trend toward decline. The benefit and power of faith-based groups is slipping away, and no one seems to care. False and insincere forms of worship have been present and recorded in both the Old and New Testaments, God declared:

> *"These people come near to me with their mouth and honor me with their lips, but their hearts are far from me. Their worship of me is based on merely human rules they have been taught. (Isaiah 29:13)*

> *"These people honor me with their lips, but their hearts are far from me."* (Matthew 15:8)

Negative Participation

A decline in weekly participation in religious activities is apparent. The lack of converts, a failure to adequately disciple the few converts, the vanishing financial resources, the public disclosure of clergy immorality, all contribute to public contempt for institutionalized religion. Not only is there growing negative participation, most faith-based groups have been unable to maintain even the existing proportion of an increasing population. Children of leaders, families of the faithful and even the poor who historically have gladly received the regular preaching of the good news, are no longer present or have turned a deaf ear to the message. Frequently the poor look to secular society and charity operations to provide for their wants.

Funding has slowly Faltered

Most efforts to increase funding for basic human needs or true missionary outreach have slowly faltered. The pattern is not the same in all faith-based groups or communities, but the tendency exists and is alarming, and it is infectious and lethal for conservative or Bible-based operations. It appears that secular and materialistic concepts and constructs have become dominate in the thinking of most churchgoers and the general public. Religious leaders are powerless to change the equation or even express concern for positive change.

The Marketplace Challenge

Traveling opens many doors for the gospel. The marketplace is the real challenge for a faith-based lifestyle, out where the people are on a daily basis. At a New York airport waiting in line for a delayed night flight, two gentlemen were in line talking around me. When they would not break line, their conversation was forced on me. Understanding their vexation, my Delta Flying Colonel card was used to take them to a more private place to wait. The Crown Room was almost deserted. Soft drinks were in the refrigerator and little fish crackers on the counter, so the munching began.

Renewal and Commitment

After a while, one asked, "*Do you work for the airline?*" A negative answer was not sufficient, the follow up question dealt with my occupation. They were told about my travels, writing and speaking. One asked, "*What do you write?*" Sharing with them about discipleship, evangelism and dying churches, one said, *"My church is spiritually dead, and I am too!"* With this the one decided to leave. Alone, God worked His mysterious process of dedication and renewal.

Involvement vs. Attendance

A note on Delta stationary from the Crown Room arrived in the mail. It listed "**Seven things God did for me today.**" Spiritual outreach is not dead; the cause of Christ is alive and well; it is just functioning better on an individual basis than it is at the institutional level. Why is this happening? Faith-based leaders and parents have failed to develop a faith-based culture that includes the practice of personal witness to God's saving grace. Local congregations must seek to enhance the quality of daily lifestyle involvement by individuals rather than attendance at a scheduled service.

A Changing Perspective

The construct *missional* clearly describes a changing perspective among Faith-based leadership. Included in this change is a refocusing on God's Word to include the real life and spiritual needs of a lost world, rather than obsessing about the unlimited materialistic wants close to home.

16. Then the eleven disciples went to Galilee, to a mountain where Jesus had arranged to meet them. 17. And when they saw Jesus, some doubted. 18. And Jesus came and spoke, saying, *All authority has been committed to Me in heaven and in earth. 19. *As you go, (going) therefore, and make disciples of all nations, baptizing them in the name of the Father, and of the Son, and of the Holy Spirit: 20. Teaching them to observe all things whatever*

I have commanded you: and, lo, I am with you always, even unto the end of the world. Amen. (Matthew 28:16-20 EDNT)

Will believers who are walking in fellowship with God and others, please take a seat at the table. Those who have been washed and cleansed have a right standing with God and have equal access to the Children's Bread.

> *9. Surely you know that the wicked shall not come into the kingdom of God. Be not deceived: neither those who live in sexual immorality, or worship idols, nor those unfaithful in marriage, nor sissy men, nor those given to sexual perversion, 10. nor thieves, **nor greed**y, nor drunkards, nor those given to slander, **nor swindlers, shall fully possess the kingdom of God**. 11. And such were some of you: **but you are washed, you are cleansed, you have a right standing with God** in the Name of the Lord Jesus, and by the Spirit of our God.* (1 Corinthians 6:9-13 EDNT)

Saint Paul demonstrated a missional lifestyle in a personal letter to the Corinthian congregation:

> *3. Habitually we give no occasion of stumbling that the ministry be discredited: 4. on the contrary, we seek to commend ourselves as God's ministers, by steadfast endurance, in troubles, in hardships, in difficulties, 5. in flogging, in bonds, in angry mobs, in hard labor, in sleepless nights, in hunger; 6. by innocence, by understanding, by long-suffering, by kindness, by the Holy Spirit, by authentic love, **7. by speaking the truth, by God's power, by weapons of righteousness, the sword of the Spirit in the right hand and the shield of faith in the left hand**,* (2 Corinthians 6:3-7 EDNT)

Paul further identified the qualities of honesty and integrity which bring prosperity to those interacting with others in the marketplace.

> *6. Be anxious for nothing; but under all circumstances by general prayer and specific petition joined with thanksgiving let your personal needs be known to God. 7. And the authentic peace of God which transcends all comprehension shall guard your hearts and minds through Christ Jesus. 8. Finally, brethren, whatever things are **genuine**, whatever things are **uncomplicated**, whatever things are **impartial**, whatever things are **unadulterated**, whatever things are **agreeable**, whatever things are **honorable**; if there be any desirable quality, and if there be any acclaim, think on these things. 9. Model your behavior on those things which you both learned and received, and seen and heard of me, practice continually: and the God of peace will be with you.* (Philippians 4:6 -9 EDNT)

The Children's Bread is available to all believers who daily take a seat at the Lord's Table and ask largely for spiritual nourishment, physical strength, family stability, guidance in consistent worship, and courage for lifestyle witnessing.

IV

Taking
A Seat At The Table

28. In Christ there is neither Jew nor Greek, bond nor free, male or female; for you are all one in Christ Jesus. 29. ***And if you belong to Christ, then you are Abraham's offspring and Abraham's promise is your promise.*** (Galatians 4:28-29 EDNT).

Promises Made to Abraham

To clearly understand God's Plan for all mankind, one must become aware of three specific promises made to Abraham in Genesis 12. **First,** God promised a specific location for Abraham and his people to live. **Second,** God promise Abraham a multitude of righteous descendants. **Thirdly,** God promised Abraham blessings that derived from the first two promises and included the whole world. However, Abraham was not promised that the fulfillment of these promises would be easy. He was told, **"Those who bless you I will bless and those who curse you I will curse."** This would mean nothing but controversy and disagreements. The real test came from the first two promises, a specific location and the righteous descendants who have constantly been harassed and troubled by evil forces.

Sequence of these Promises

It is important to see that the sequence of all these promises continue into the New Testament. The Jewish Messiah became Redeemer of all mankind in the New Testament and continues as the Deliverer and cure and care of troubled souls throughout history into the present. This means that Gentiles are included in Abraham's promises before the foundation of the world. Although God went to the Jews first, He never intended to leave Gentiles out of His Promises.

> *4. before the foundation of the world He chose us in Christ, that we should be consecrated and blameless before Him in love: 5. having planned beforehand for our adoption to Himself by Jesus Christ, according to the good pleasure of His will,* (Galatians 6:4-5 EDNT)

> *19. Therefore* **you are no more outsiders, but fellow citizens with the saints, and belong to the household of God; 20. and are now built on the foundation of the prophets and the apostles, Jesus Christ Himself being the foundation stone;** *(Ephesians 2:19-20 EDNT)*

However, the inclusion of Gentiles in these promises would mean that Gentiles would also suffer opposition in the fulfilment of God's Plan:

> **1. And Saul with pleasure gave formal consent to Stephen's death. And great persecution broke out against the believers in Jerusalem** (Acts 8:1 EDNT)

> *7. But we have this treasure in earthen vessels that the all-prevailing greatness of the power may be of God, and not from us.* **8. We are pressed on every**

side, yet not hemmed in, we are bewildered, but never at a loss; 9. persecuted, but not abandoned; knocked down, but never counted out; 10. always exposed to the dying of the body. (2 Corinthians 4:7-10 EDNT) *12. Now I would have you to understand, that which I have gone through will most likely advance the gospel; 13. so that my chains in Christ are known in all the praetorian guard and all the palace; 14. and many of the brethren have gained confidence by my chains and are more fluent to speak the word with courage.* (Philippians 1:12-14 EDNT) *12. Yes, all who will live godly lives in Christ Jesus will be persecuted.* (2 Timothy 3:12 EDNT) *12. My dearly loved brothers, do not think the test by fire kindling about you is some strange thing happening only to you.* (1 Peter 4:12-14 EDNT)

Difficulties Relate to God's Promises

Understanding God's plan and the controversy among nations requires one to see that these difficulties relate to God's three promises to Abraham and that God is committed to fulfill them through the Person of His Son. Through repentance and Faith-based worship, all believers have a seat at the Lord's Table. This is the place in God's s Grace that requires confession of sin, mercy, and obtaining righteousness through the Redeemer. When believers are considered the righteous descendants of Abraham, and Jesus has His rightful place in the hearts and minds of converts, those individuals have a seat at the Lord's Table with access to the Children's Bread and all the blessings of Mercy and Grace promised to Abraham.

*26. **For we are all the children of God by faith in Christ Jesus.** 27. For as many as have been identified with Christ by baptism have been clothed with the attributes of Christ. 28. **In Christ there is neither Jew nor Greek, bond nor free, male or female; for you are all one in Christ Jesus. 29.** <u>**And if you belong to Christ, then you are Abraham's offspring and Abraham's promise is your promise.**</u>* (Galatians 3:26-29 EDNT) **18. For through Him we both have the right of entry to the Father's promises by one Spirit.** (Ephesians 2:18 EDNT)

God's Plan

Sacred Scripture affirms that the Hebrew People were chosen by God for a specific purpose. (Deuteronomy 7:6). It is obvious that God had a plan: He chose a man to begin a family; He chose that family to become a Nation; He enabled that Nation to produce the Messiah for all people. Early on it was clear that the Redeemer would come through the line of Abraham, Isaac, and Jacob and then the Messiah's ancestry was narrowed to the line of David. The Bible bears witness that directly and indirectly Jesus was to bring both Jews and Gentiles together. 18. *For through Him we both have the right of entry to the Father's promises by one Spirit.* (Ephesians 2:14 EDNT) This gives all justified believers a seat at the table and access to the children's bread.

Kitchen Table and the Family

According to sacred scripture, God made the family the basic structure of society and the building stones for the faith-based worship of the Supreme Being. The family was designed to produce, protect, and preserve individuals in the context of their primary institutions.   Individuals are **produced** in the family; **protected** in the community; and **preserved** in Faith-based entities with which the family is connected. The family and those who comprise the whole must be given priority for any endeavor to be in harmony with the Creator. This makes the kitchen table a valuable asset in child and family growth and development. Thus, we have a primary concept for family leadership: *"If anyone provides not for his own people, and especially his family, he has denied the faith, and is worse than an unbeliever."* (1 Timothy 5:8 EDNT)

> 18. All things are of God, who has brought us together in Himself by Jesus Christ, and has given to us the ministry of bringing people together; 19. how that God was in Christ bringing together the world to Himself, not counting their false steps and blunders against them; and has committed us to speak intelligent words that bring man and God together. 20. Now seeing we are representatives for Christ, as though God did make His appeal through us: we implore you in Christ's stead, come together with God. *(2 Corinthians 5:18-20 EDNT)*

Theology of the Kitchen Table

Is there a theological construct for the family table? A realization of this truth was awakened some years ago visiting a small congregation in Minneapolis. When I or my family traveled without a scheduled preaching appointment, it was the custom to worship with the closest congregation to where we

slept on Saturday evening. Attending an academic
meeting in Minnesota, my wife and I worshiped
with a small Presbyterian Church near the motel. It
was the first sermon for the new minister and his
message was: *"The Theology of the Kitchen Table."*
He proceeded to explain his philosophy of ministry
in connection with the kitchen table: that family and
close friends ate at the kitchen table, but guests,
visitors, and strangers were normally served in the
dining room.

God's Kitchen

The young Pastor wanted the membership to
consider the sanctuary to be God's Kitchen where
family and friends could gather for support and
nourishment. He made it clear that his philosophy
of ministry opened the door for visitors, guests,
and strangers and that he expected the faithful
membership to build a relationship with these until
they became as "family or dear friends" and could
be nourished with them in God's Kitchen. His goal
was that everyone would have a seat at the kitchen
table. In the minister's view, there was always a seat
for everyone in God's Kitchen with access to the
Children's Bread.

Impact of the Gospel

In Matthew 24, Jesus declared the gospel must
impact every tribe and tongue and become a blessing
to all the nations of the world. In Acts 1, Jesus taught
His apostles about full restoration of the Kingdom
of God and that His followers were to be witnesses

unto the death to spread the Good News of Mercy and Grace to all people through a missional witness by called and committed believers. In Galatians, the ultimate fulfilment by Jesus of the promises given to Abraham, are presented. Hebrews 11, Abraham and others did not receive the full promise, because God planned for Gentiles believers to be included in the original promises God made to Abraham and his seed.

> *39. And these all, having obtained a good report through faith, received not the promise: 40.* **For us, God had something better in store. We were needed, to make the history of their lives complete.** (Hebrews 11:32-40 EDNT) *14. Just as Moses lifted up the serpent in the wilderness, even so must the Son of Man be lifted up: 15 that whoever believes may have in Him eternal life. 16.* **For God so loved the world that He gave His only begotten Son, that whoever believes in Him should not perish, but have everlasting life.** *17. For God sent not His Son into the world to judge the world;* **but that the world through Him might be saved.** (John 3: 14-18 EDNT)

The Just shall live by Faith

> *15. As far as I am able, I am ready to preach the gospel to you at Rome also. 16. For* **I am never reluctant to preach the gospel: for it is the power of God unto salvation to all who believe; to the Jew first, and also to the Greek. 17. For in the gospel God reveals His worthy activity that begins and ends with faith: the permanent and authoritative character of the written Word affirms, the just shall live by faith.** (Romans 1:11-17 EDNT)

A Seat "not a place" at the Table

There is a difference between a place at the table and a seat at the table. The Hebrew nation had a "place" assigned at the table but individually refused to take their seat. A "place" is an assigned chair with a name on it, while a seat at the table means you are welcome but you must accept the invitation, take initiative and find an open seat. Saving grace opens the table for all who are born-again believer walking in fellowship with the Lord. The Children's Bread is available to all God's Children; believers do not have to be satisfied with scraps that fall from the table. In the dispensation of Grace, God does not assign seats at His table; He simply has enough seats for all His children. Not only does God promise redemption, but Jesus instructed His followers to seek for "daily bread," through employment. Earning bread by sweat is still an operational injunction. It is clear that one does not live by material or financial "bread" alone, but must also be sustained by the Word of God and the promised blessings inscribed in the Word:

> **9.** Honor the LORD with your wealth, with the first fruits of all your crops; *10* then your barns will be filled to overflowing, and your vats will brim over with new wine. (Proverbs 3:9-10 NIV)

Believe and Behave

Provided you believe and behave in a manner that maintains fellowship with God, you are welcome at God's Table and there is *"enough and then some"* of the Children's Bread for all those in good standing with some left over for the poor and needy who gladly hear the Good News that proceeds from the places of worship and the continuing lifestyle testimony of the faithful.

6. Remember the saying, he who sows in a miserly manner shall reap miserly; and he who sows generously shall reap an abundant harvest. 7. Let every man give as he purposed in his heart; not reluctantly or under constraint: for God loves a prompt and willing giver. 8. Now God is continually able to overflow you with self-sufficiency always making you competent to pour out to the good of others: 9. As it is written, his generosity is scattered to the poor; his love-deeds are never forgotten. 10. **Now he who supplies plenty of seed for the planting also furnishes bread for your table, and multiplies the seed sown and increases the fruit of your benevolence; 11. Your being enriched unto all liberality causes us to give thanks to God. 12. The rendering of this benevolence not only supplies the needs of the saints but causes a wealth of thanksgiving to God; 13. By evidence of this service they glorify God for your conviction and response to the gospel of Christ and for your liberality in sharing with others;** *14. and by their intercession for you their earnest desire goes out to you to surpass your grace and generosity. 15. Thanks to God for his indescribable generosity to you.* (2 Corinthians 9:6-15 EDNT)

The Problems of Grafting

From the teaching of the Old Testament, the Jewish people had a specific system to guide their understanding about wealth and support of the Temple, the Priest, and the advancement of God's righteous cause. Gentiles, on the other hand, were permitted a seat at the table without the longstanding background and teachings concerning God's economy and personal wealth. This is part of the problem with Faith-based operations today. They take from the root, but do not give back. They become takers and not givers.

> *11. Remember your nature as Gentiles, that you did not physically conform to the Jewish tradition; 12. that you were without Christ, being outside the commonwealth of Israel, and outside the covenants of promise, without hope, and without God in the world:* **13. but now in Christ Jesus you who were outside are brought inside the promises by the blood of Christ. 14. For He is the bond of peace that unites both parts into one having dissolved the partition between us;** (Ephesians 2:11-13 EDNT)

Rights to the Children's Bread

All who belong to Christ have been offered a seat at the Lord's Table with rights to the Children's Bread and no longer need to scramble for crumbs. This means that Gentiles have been included or "grafted" into God's Plan and should appreciate the foundation stones laid down by the prophets, priests, and kings of the past as recorded in sacred Scripture. There is a difference in a "place" and a "seat" at the table. God does not designate a particular seat with a place card: God's table has open seating. You must take a seat at the table using your own initiative. It is true, the Jewish Nation was offered a seat at the table first, but once they refused to take their seat it was offered to Gentile converts. God always planned to graft Gentiles into the Olive Tree of Redemption. This was God's plan before the foundation of the universe. Yet, Gentiles being grafted have a special place in the kingdom: equal before God but blessed in a different way. History clearly informs the world what God does with those who reject His invitation to take a seat at His table. Paul made it clear to the Romans that the exclusion of the Jews for a time meant the inclusion of the world in salvation, and that his hope was the Jews would be restored a place of honor. Meanwhile, the rest of the world was now enjoying the full blessings of God.

16. When the first loaf is holy: the whole batch is consecrated: and if the root of the tree is holy, so are the branches. 17. And if some branches were broken off, and you being of a wild olive tree were grafted into the tree and became also a partaker of the root and richness of the olive tree; 18. you must not look down on the branches that were broken off, but remember you do not support the root, the root supports you. **19. You may say, the branches were broken off that I might be grafted into the tree. 20. But it was from lack of faith that they were broken off, and you stand in their place by faith. Stop being proud but be on guard: 21. for if God spared not the natural branches, pay attention lest He also not spare you.** *22. Consider both the kindness and strict justice of God: on them who fell, strict justice; but toward you, kindness, if you continue steadfast in His goodness; otherwise you will also be pruned from the tree. 23. And should they not remain in unbelief, God is able to graft them in again.* **24. For if you were cut out of a** *wild olive tree and grafted contrary to nature into a good olive tree: how much more shall these, who are the natural branches, be grafted into their own olive tree? 25. For I would not have you ignorant of this hidden truth, lest you deceive yourselves; that a partial hardening has befallen Israel, until the full number of Gentiles come to faith.* (Romans 11:16-25 EDNT)

Sub-contracted Task

God has continued to bless His chosen people Israel, but they have not financed the expansion of the Messiah's work on earth. That task has been sub-contracted to the Gentile converts and to their places of worship. This should call attention to the serious issue of understanding kingdom economy and personal wealth that is designed to support families and the outreach enterprises of the kingdom.

Gentiles must fulfill this obligation, or they too will be rejected from the source of wealth and prosperity. Paul explained in Romans 11 about the conceited and egotistical perspective of the Gentiles who have been *grafted into the tree and became also a partaker of the root and richness of the olive tree.* This made the grafted branch a *"taker without giving"* a kind of parasite or freeloader taking but never giving back.

The Problem of Sectarian Fruit

The character of a grafted branch illustrated the idea. Paul said, *"You do not support the root, but the root supports you."* A grafted branch does not support the root, which nourishes its life, but the root supports the engrafted branch. The grafted branch may live, grow, produce foliage and even fruit, but remains an unorthodox part of the larger unit. It often becomes militant and radical and is a liability to the original unit. The graft may also become a hindrance to growth and fruit bearing by sapping strength from the source. This may explain the advance of multiple denominations and many independent faith-based groups which operate by taking strength from the root of Christianity, but uses the source to make their own sectarian fruit without supporting the basic foundation stones of the Faith. This has become a detriment to Christianity and a limiting factor in advancing the Kingdom of God on earth.

Yellow Apples on a Red Apple Tree

In my Grandfather Green's front yard was a small red apple tree, but one of the branches produced a yellowish apple. I was curious, so he explained that the branch producing the yellow apple was grafted into the red apple tree. Fascinated I asked, *"How do you do that? How does it work?"* With great patience Grandfather explained the process of splitting the branches in a specific way and placing them together. He showed me about binding them together tightly with twine and covering the whole joined area with bee's wax and shared that the grafting process was limited because the new branch was a "taker" and not a "giver."

The Supply System Problem

Nature nourishes fruit-bearing trees with a supply of a watery liquid called sap. It moves upward in part through an intricate supply system. It seems for the most part the grafted branch sucks nourishment from the roots of the host tree, but it does not give anything back. Other branches assist the tree through sap-lifting forces by evaporation and transpiration. This is a kind of breathing water through the leaves. The grafted branch does not give anything back; it is a kind of freeloader living off the energy or vitality of the root without giving anything back to the tree.

The Weakening of Christianity

The grafted branch uses all the sunshine and rain on its leaves to produce its own apples of different variety and colors. It is a strain on the original tree, because the grafted branch actually takes sap away from the other branches bearing red apples. Too many grafts and they would suck the life out of a tree in the process of producing apples. Perhaps this explains about the weakening of Christianity: One Lord, One Faith, One Baptism, but multiple denominations and local faith-based groups behaving as "grafted" branches pulling life out of the roots of Christianity and the Word without giving back adequate support for the general Cause. There is little substance given back to the root of Christianity that produces a moral lifestyle and advances the Kingdom. Most seem to be interest in the apples on their branch with little concern with nourishment for the tree that enabled them to live and produce fruit.

A Learned Lesson

It was a learned lesson about *"givers and taker"* and realized that most of us at some time or the other may be on both ends of that ambiguity. Takers should work at giving, and givers should not begrudge their giving. Scripture is clear, *"It is more blessed to give than to receive."* It must be understood that a life of Christian service and missional living is one of giving not taking. This philosophy should permeate the life of mature believers and assist their knowledge of growing Faith-based families, doing basic evangelism, and the planting and growing congregations and Faith-based groups as well as larger institutions which directly advance the Kingdom.

Foliage without Fruit

An understanding of the concept of grafting may clarify the problem as it relates to the integration of communities. One does not have to be a horticulturist to see the disadvantage of foliage without fruit or different kinds of fruit growing on the same tree. Such groups become "takers" without giving a fair share commitment to the infrastructure, which forms the basis for their existence. It is similar to privileged entitlement and extended dependence on government handouts which one receives but pays little of the cost.

16. When the first loaf is holy: the whole batch is consecrated: and if the root of the tree is holy, so are the branches. 17. And if some branches were broken off, and you being of a wild olive tree were grafted into the tree and became also a partaker of the root and richness of the olive tree; 18. you must not look down on the branches that were broken off, but remember you do not support the root, the root supports you. (Romans 11: 16-18 EDNT)

Little is Accomplished

My firm belief is that many churchgoers simply take and never really give back in time, talent, tithe, or true worship that demonstrates the "worth-ship" of God in their lives. Not only are they part of congregations that reach back to the tap root of the New Testament for support but builds their own tradition filled with "do's and don'ts" and little gets done for the Kingdom. Most of their resources are poured back into staff, programs, buildings, and showy community projects to enhance their public position. Little is accomplished to win the lost, assist the poor, reach out to the neighborhood, or advance the message of grace globally. The buildings remained locked, except for scheduled meetings, and little concern is shown for those who live in the neighborhood.   The only "service" produced is the scheduled worship or activities and meetings; of which, some are called *services*. Often the attendees feel they have done God a "service" and no further effort is required until later, maybe next week. This is the reality of being a "**taker not a giver**" or only accepting the "blessing" of receiving and avoiding the cost of "giving."

Advance Humanity and True Religion

Provided everyone clearly understood the problems of grafting the material and spiritual aspects of Faith-based operations would be more effective. An individual or a group cannot long take from the nourishing roots of Christianity and use sacred scripture to their own advantage without giving back unreserved loyalty and support for the global cause of Christ and the needs of world evangelism. In the past, I authored seven (7) books dealing with this matter: *Discipleship, Why Churches Die, Why Wait Till Sunday? Why Christianity Fails in America, Titanic Lessons, Fighting the Amalekites, and Tear Down These Walls.* Little has changed in the past five decades. Kingdom economics and personal wealth are still limited by "takers" who fail to "give back" of themselves, their resources, and time through a missional lifestyle. The basic needs of the poor, who once listened to the Gospel willingly, now depend on government and charity for their daily needs. They are not made into disciples or taught to work for their "daily bread" as Jesus instructed and do share God's blessings with others to advance basic humanity and true religion.

> 5. On an occasion, the Pharisees asked Jesus, *Why do your disciples not walk according to the tradition of the elders, but eat bread with unwashed hands? 6. He answered, you hypocrites, Isaiah prophesied and described you, **This people honors me with their lips, but their heart is far from me. 7. Their worship is empty, teaching for doctrines the precepts of men. 8. You give up what God commanded and cling to your own tradition…making the word of God of none effect through your tradition.***
> (Mark 7:5-13 EDNT*)*

Unoccupied Seats at the Lord's Table

Notwithstanding, we have a seat at the Lord's Table with access to God's unlimited supply, many still scramble for the "crumbs" of material wealth and fail to reap the benefits of the Children's Bread and Kingdom Economics. Most believers live far beneath their privilege as a Child of God with a seat at the Lord's Table. There are many unoccupied seats at the table and those failing to take their seat must scramble for the "scraps" that fall from the table. Believers, their families, and Kingdom support deserve more.

A Sense of Entitlement

One fact to remember: God has not rescinded His declaration that *"daily bread comes by the sweat of work."* A Seat at the Table of Providence does not eliminate the need for work or to assume responsibility for debts and normal obligations of family life. The blessings of the Kingdom do not eliminate the necessity of physical labor. In fact, an early concept about bread and work was established when God told Adam. *"You will earn your bread by the sweat of your brow."* Secular and materialistic leaders have created a sense of entitlement and caused many to expect handouts from charity and government as a "right" rather than temporary assistance for short-term needs. Sadly, some religious leaders have propagated a "gold, glory, and glamor" philosophy and cause some to believe that their gifts to the Kingdom is a guarantee to prosperity rather than an opportunity to share in assisting others and advancing the Kingdom. Some converts and secular saints expect the generosity of God's bounty to provide all their wants, when God's blessings are promised to those who faithfully walk in fellowship with Christ and others. Certainly, there are some, who must receive assistance from Faith-based groups and government entities, but it is not a right or entitlement; caring for the basic needs of those unable to care for themselves is a basic tenant of humanity and most religions. This is not an obligation to enable and empower able-bodied individuals who refuse to work for their daily bread.

The Great Leveler

The faith-based way of life should be a force to unite rather than a wall to divide the family. In Christ, there are no first and second-string teams; no one-man shows; no single voice choirs, no one deacon run church, no big "I" and/or little "you;" according to Galatians 3:28 no rich or poor... Christianity levels the field of labor and all stand equal before God and are required to earn daily bread by labor. Yes, Jesus told His disciples to *"pray for daily bread"* leveling playing field. The human factor or cultural limitation should not be allowed to complicate the universal values of the faith-based agenda. Everyone must seek to follow the one Right Path to the gates of Heaven by taking their seat at the Lord's Table and sharing the blessings and fellowship with others.

Made of Acacia Wood

Jewish history notes that three of the main vessels of the Temple – the table, the ark, and the altar were all made out of acacia wood. The early Rabbis made an acronym of acacia, translated into English meaning. *peace, goodness, salvation, and forgiveness.* Acacia is hardwood suitable for building long-lasting items of furniture. It is water-resistant, attractive in color and grain. God selects and accepts things that have beauty, functionality, and endurance whether it is wood for Temple furniture or a spiritual leader called for service.

Vehicle of Blessings

After the destruction of the Temple in 70 CE, tables in homes for the Jewish People became the vehicle to bring about blessings to family and friends. The gathering around the family table was for nourishment, fellowship, friendship, and spiritual celebration. The Hebrew word for table is *shulchan,* meaning "of grace." The table is a place of grace where we are blessed and where we bless others. As we share food, warmth, and create a welcoming atmosphere, we receive God's blessings.

> *46. And they agreed to meet daily in the temple and to break bread from house to house, and they took meals cheerfully and with personal commitment. 47. Praising God and having favor with all the people.* **And the Lord added to the church daily those being saved.** *(Acts 2:446-47 EDNT)*

Keys to Unlocking Kingdom Thinking

9. Let love be without hypocrisy. Hate what is wrong. Cleave to the good. 10. Have tender affection for the believers; go before one another as an honorable guide; 11. do not delay your enthusiasm; be on fire in the spirit; serving the Lord as a slave; 12. rejoice in hope; remain steadfast in time of trouble; be persistent in the habit of prayer; 13. ***contribute your share with reference to the needs of the saints; give attention to hospitality.*** (Romans 12:9-13 EDNT)

Why is the gate locked? Who has the keys to the kingdom? Who knows how to unlock the secrets of kingdom economics and personal wealth?

1. And Jesus observed the rich men placing their gifts into the treasury. 2. Also He saw a poor widow putting in two small coins. 3. And said, Truly this poor widow has given more that everyone: 4. for the wealthy gave out of their abundance: but she out of her scarcity has put in her whole living.

(Luke 21:1-4 EDNT)

V

Unlocking
Kingdom Thinking

13. "A good man leaves an inheritance [of moral stability and goodness] to his children's children, but the wealth of the owner is stored up for [the hands of] the righteous." (Proverbs 13:22 (EDOT) *10.* His children must make amends to the poor; his own hands must give back his wealth. (Job 20:10 NIV) *10. For all can see that the wise die, that the foolish and the senseless also perish, leaving their wealth to others.* (Psalm 49:10 NIV)

Symbolism of a Key

A key is a symbol of freedom, a tool that permits the opening of locked doors. There are many locked doors that prohibit entry to certain people. A locked door can be a form of privacy and security or a symbol of power to control certain aspects of the lives of others. When it comes to money matters and personal wealth there seems to be a giant padlock on the door to wealth and a combination lock on the gate to prosperity. The question is where can the keys to the financial padlock be found and where in the world is the combination code for the lock on the gate to prosperity?

First, one must unlock kingdom thinking about prosperity and God's user-friendly approach to wealth found in His sixty-six (66) book library. The entry card is free but requires effort to find the needed data and learn to properly use the knowledge. This book is an effort to find scriptural guides to the keys to kingdom economics designed to assist the family, community, and the faith-based entities who seek to advance God's will on earth and fund humanitarian efforts to assist the poor and needed identified as pure religion. The combination code to the lock on the gate to personal wealth and prosperity is hidden in Kingdom thinking for each individual to discover by taking a seat at the Lord's Table and gaining access to the Children's Bread.

Daily Bread

Established in the Garden, the concept of *"earning daily bread by the sweat of the brow"* has not been rescinded. This remains God's plan of supplying the required *"daily bread"* for mankind. Faith without works is dead orthodoxy and will not put bread on the table, feed the hungry or provide shelter for the homeless. When the Proverb declared that wealth is stored for the *"hands"* of the righteous, it suggests we all must work for the funds we need to both support the family and advance the Kingdom. *That the wealth of the sinner is stored up for **the hands of the righteous**, the meaning is obvious. When someone invests and opens a business to provide employment for others who must use their "hands" and work for wages, this scripture is being fulfilled.*

Economics of the Kingdom

When believers seek gold, glory, and glamour using the money-oriented route their wealth and fame are acquired through a secular mindset and a materialistic economy. However, when one "**seeks first the kingdom of God**" the economics of the kingdom works to their benefit and more specifically the benefaction of others.

> *32. Fear not, little flock; for it is your Father's good pleasure to give you the kingdom. 33. Keep your assets liquid and give alms; provide yourselves a purse that does not grow old, a treasure in the heavens that fails not, where no thief has access, neither moths can spoil. 34. For where your treasure is, there your heart will be also.* (Luke 12:32-34 EDNT)

Rich Man's Quandary

> *20. And he answered, Master, all these have I obeyed from my youth. 21. When Jesus observed him clearly, He loved Him, and said, One thing you lack: go sell you possessions and give the funds to the poor, and you shall have treasure in heaven: and come back and follow Me. 22. And he was depressed at the request and went away with great sadness: for he had much property.* (Mark 10:20-22 EDNT)

Provided one reads between the lines: *[And Jesus let him go.]* Individuals must decide whether or not they will participate in God's Plan. God's love and care alone is not enough for personal prosperity, there must be willing participation.

> *7. And John said to the crowds that came to be baptized, you brood of snakes, who has prompted you to seek refuge from the coming punishment? 8. Then*

produce fruits consistent with your repentance, *and do not begin to say, we have Abraham as our father:* **for I say, that God is able to raise up children to Abraham out of these stones.** *9. Also the axe is laid at the root of the trees: every tree that does not produce good fruit is cut down and cast into the fire. 10. And the people asked him,* **what shall we do** *then? 11. He answered them,* **He that has two coats, let him share with him that has none; and he that has food, let him do likewise.** *12. Then, tax-collectors came to be baptized, and asked, Master,* **what shall we do?** *13. And he said unto them,* **collect only the prescribed amount.** *14. And the soldiers likewise demanded of him, saying, And* **what shall we do?** *And John said unto them,* **Do violence to no man, neither accuse any falsely; and be content with your wages.** *Luke 3:7-14 EDNT)*

When the System Works

God works through the system when the system works. There are divine rules for living and giving; this includes the process of having access to the Children's Bread and the gathering of "*more than enough*" to care for the family, the poor, and kingdom endeavors. When one has "*more than enough*," God has designated material things (including money) for charity and kingdom activities. Caring for the poor, the sick, the homeless, and the needs of Kingdom ministries and workers. Those who witness near their home and those who journey into a strange place to share the Good News following the leadership of the Holy Spirit. One thing is clear: God works through the system when the system works. The explanation of the rich man and the beggar tells part of the story of how God works through the system…when the system works:

> *19. There was a certain rich man who usually dressed in purple and fine linen and feasted daily in luxury: 20. and a beggar named Lazarus, was laid at the rich man's gate, whose skin was full of boils. 21. Desiring to be fed with the crumbs from the rich man's table: only the dogs licked his sores to aid healing. 22. But the beggar died and was taken by angels to Abraham's bosom: the rich man died also and was buried; 23. and from the habitation of the dead he saw Abraham at a distance and Lazarus in his arms.* 24. And he cried, Father Abraham, have mercy on me and send Lazarus that he may dip his finger in water and cool my tongue; for I am in anguish here. 25. But Abraham said, Son**, remember in your lifetime you received the good things, and likewise Lazarus the misfortunes of life: but now he is comforted, and you are in anguish.** *26. And beside this, between us there is a great fixed chasm: so that none who wish may pass either way. 27. Then the rich man said, I pray you, father, send Lazarus to my father's house: 28. for I have five brothers: that he may witness to them lest they come to this place of torment. 29.* Abraham said, They have Moses and the prophets, let them hear them. 30. And he said, **No father Abraham: but if one went from the dead they would repent. 31. And Abraham said, If they hear not Moses and the prophets, neither would they be persuaded though one stood up from the grave.** (Luke 16:19-31 EDNT)

More of the story is found in an account of Ten Lepers who were examples of God working through the system…when the system works.

12. At the entrance of a certain village, ten lepers met Him and stood at a distance: 13. And called to Him, Jesus, Master, have mercy on us. 14. And when He saw them, He said, **Go show yourselves to the priests. And as they went, they were cured.** *15. <u>One of them, when he saw he was healed, turned back, and glorifying God with a loud voice, 16. and fell prostrate at his feet, giving Jesus thanks: and he was a Samaritan.</u> 17. And Jesus asked, Were there not ten cleansed? But where are the nine? * 18.* **We find only this foreigner who returned to give glory to God. 19. And Jesus said, Arise, go your way, your faith has made you whole.** (Luke 17:11-19 EDNT)

———————

*v17 The nine were obeying Jesus and on their way to show themselves to the priests. Since the Samaritan was not allowed in the Temple, he returned to show his appreciation directly to Jesus. It appears that **God works through the system, when the system works.**

Hard Work Ends in Profit

A good man is a hard worker and diligent in business; manual labor has its rough, unpleasant side, yet hard work is the God ordained route to legitimate funding. In a workshop for the Washington, DC Chamber of Commerce, the trainer summarized his class by saying, *"One may work hard all day and have a bad day or work hard all week and have a bad week,* **but no one who works hard all month will have a bad month."** It is the good businessmen and the hard work of good men that are able to care for their family and others and still leave an inheritance to the children. It becomes clear from the scripture that those who acquire their wealth without working or through *"unearned income"* do not take their gains with them because they are stored for the working hands of the righteous. Exactly how this happens is a mystery, but it happens just the same. One way -- the rich create a business and hire workers to produce a product and the worker is paid wages for the labor with his hands and mind.

Honest Work for Honest Pay

All who take a seat at the table are eligible for this windfall. This is not gold and glory for the glamorous, but hard work to acquire a portion of the invested wealth stored for the worker worthy of wages. Honest work for honest pay is a spiritual exercise which fulfills God's declaration that one must *"earn their bread by the sweat of labor."* Hard work is the scriptural procedure for acquiring personal income to support both the family and finance humanitarian operations and kingdom endavors. Note this proverb, ***Dishonest money dwindles away, but whoever gathers money little by little makes it grow"***. *(Proverbs 13:11 NIV)* Earning money by working steadily, paycheck by paycheck, is an honest route to basic prosperity. Many are not willing to live a life worthy of the benefit!

Keys and Title

Here is a personal story of a friend, Subesh Ramjattan, who began working for a shoe company operated by a man from India. Each Saturday Subesh volunteered to wash and clean the owner's Volkswagen. After three years of washing the VW, the owner decided to retire and move back to India. The keys to the VW along with the title were handed to the **car washer** as a gift. Subesh was a young believer and treated the transaction as a spiritual gift –a true blessing from God. It was a validation of Proverbs 13:22 *"the wealth of the owner is stored up for [for the hands of] the righteous."* Three years of working on his day off and by hand cleaning and washing the owner's car was a fulfilment of by *"the hands of"* the righteous the wealth was passed. The rewards of honest labor are unlimited. Proverbs 11:30 *"he that wins souls is wise"* and James 1:5 relate the matter of wisdom to soul-winning and associates being wise to experiencing joy and gladness. (See Philippians 2:1-11 EDNT)

> *3. knowing that your painful trial brings you assurance, trust and works patience. 4. But let suffering have her complete labor and make something of you, that you may be complete in all respects, without defect or omission and whole undivided, and unbroken. 5. If any of you lack wise judgment, let him express the craving by words to God, that gives to all men liberally, and does not defame, chide or snatch away your joy, and it shall be given him. 6. but let him ask in faith, nothing wavering, for he that shows doubt or indecision is like a wave of the sea driven with the wind and tossed. **7. let not that man think that he shall receive any thing of the Lord. 8. a two-spirited man is unsettled and wavering in all his direction, position or manner. 9. let the brother of low degree experience joy and gladness that he is exalted. 10.** But the rich are depressed in pride and dignity because as the flower of grass shall pass*

away. 11. for the sun is no sooner near a vertical position with a burning heat, but it withers the grass, and the flower thereof falls, and the grace of the shape or figure of it perishes so also shall the rich man be extinguished and withers in his ways. (James 1:3 -11 EDNT)

Making Disciples is a Process

The process of making disciples is sequential and occurs over time; it is not a one-shot event. First, an individual becomes convicted of sin by the Holy Spirit through the Word of a witness (*a convict agrees with the verdict*). Hearing the Word, they are convinced by their own conscience (John 8; Psalms 32:1-2). One who agrees with the word that they are lost becomes "convicted" of sin and confesses to God, and then becomes a learner to grow in grace and knowledge (this is disciple making). As disciples mature they are trusted with the message and become ambassadors or envoy or some would call them apostles. Ambassadors are "accredited" based on knowledge and behavior and recognized by others as a confirmed apostle or representative of a Higher Authority.

The New Testament equivalent of ambassador is apostle, a recognized messenger with a lifestyle and the capacity to represent the message of kingdom to others, because *they are attentive to the needs of others, affectionate, gentle, concerned, considerate, and compassionate.*

To summarize this process:

1. The Holy Spirit through the Word brings an individual under conviction of sin. When they agree with the verdict and confess their sin they become a CONVERT.

2. As a convert grows in grace and knowledge through the guidance and mentorship of other believers, they become a "learner" or DISCIPLE. This is "disciple making."

3. As DISCIPLES mature they become selected or entrusted with the message of grace and become an Ambassador of the Kingdom of Heaven and a personal representative of Jesus to the lost world; thus, the biblical equivalent of ambassador is APOSTLE.

4. An apostle is one sent with a message; therefore, a witness and the biblical word for witness is *martyr one whose lifestyle causes a willingness to suffer as a witness for a cause.*

*And for one whole year they assembled with the church and taught many people. And the **disciples first began to be called* (transact their affairs) as Christians in Antioch.** 27. At this time prophets from Jerusalem came to Antioch. 28. And one of them came forward named Agabus and predicted by the Spirit that a famine was to visit the whole world: and it did happen in the time of Claudius. **29. Then every disciple according to his ability determined to send relief to the brethren in Judea:** 30. This they did and sent it to the elders by Barnabas and Saul. (Acts 11:26-30 EDNT)*

___* [The Greek word translated in KJV as "called" originally meant "to transact business" or "to have dealings with." After one whole year, the public began to recognize the difference in those being taught by Paul and Barnabas. At first it was a life-style recognized by others;

then it became a mark of identification as a follower of Christ. The Disciples did not assume the name themselves; it was a recognition by others of their missional lifestyle.]

> *Finally, brothers, we urge you in the Lord Jesus, that, as you have received instructions from us as to **how you must behave to please God, so you should follow the pattern more and more.** 2. For you know the instructions we gave you through the Lord Jesus; 3. For this is the will of God, even your separation from sexual immorality and that you resist fornication: 4. Each one of you must learn to control the sensual impulses that are natural in the body and do it with honor; 5. Not as the natural urge toward carnal desires as the Gentiles do in their ignorance of God: 6. **None of you should be excessive, and take advantage of his brother in business dealings. Because the Lord is the avenger of such excess, as our testimony forewarned you.** 7. For God did not call us to impurity but to consecration. 8 Therefore he who rejects this instruction does not reject man, but rejects the God who gave us the Holy Spirit.* (1 Thessalonians 4:1-8 EDNT)

> *9. Let love be without hypocrisy. Hate what is wrong. Cleave to the good. 10. Have tender affection for the brotherhood; go before one another as an honorable guide; **11. Do not *delay your enthusiasm; be on fire in the spirit; serving the Lord as a slave;** 12. rejoice in hope; remain steadfast in time of trouble; be persistent in the habit of prayer; 13. **contribute your share with reference to the needs of the saints;** give attention to hospitality. 14. Bless all who persecute you: bless and curse not. 15. Share the happiness of those who rejoice and share the sorrow of those who are sad. 16. Maintain harmony with one another. Set your mind on high things but accept*

humble ways. Do not think too highly of yourself. 17. Never pay back injury for injury. Aim to do what is honorable in the sight of all men. 18. As much as you can, live peaceable with all men. 19. Never avenge yourselves dearly beloved but leave room for Gods anger: for it is written, vengeance is mine; I will repay, said the Lord. 20. There is another test, if your enemy hunger, feed him; if he thirsts, give him drink: for in so doing you will make him feel a burning sense of shame. 21. Never permit evil to conquer you but get the better of evil by doing good. (Romans 129-21 EDNT)

-----

* The KJB rendered vs 11 **not slothful in business**; fervent in spirit; serving the Lord; However, in vs 11 the Greek rendering suggest: idle, lazy, troublesome. But Josephus used the same word in reference to **military attacks** which slowed down because those fighting became soft and lost heart. (Jos., JW,4:584).

Problem is the Use of Wealth

When we recognize wealth as the gift of God, we understand that it comes from God and belongs to God. This is a difficult position for most humans to adopt. But sacred scripture makes it clear that God created everything, God sustains everything, and God owns everything. Psalm 104:24 declared, *"The earth is full of your possessions."* In 1 Chronicles 29:11 it is recorded, *"Yours, O LORD, is the greatness, the power and the glory, the victory and the majesty; for all that is in heaven and in earth is yours."* Haggai 2:8 declared, *"'The silver is Mine, and the gold is Mine,' says the LORD of Hosts."* Everything in the ground, everything above the ground, everything in the air, everything that passes through the air ultimately belongs to God. **Unless wealth is managed by scriptural principles it has no solid foundation.** Wealth or money is not the problem, but it is the attitude, the predisposition or mindset that determines how money is used that creates the difficulty.

A Lack of Control

The difficult is not past debt or future liabilities, it is a lack of control at the moment of decision when cost is determined. Sufficient to the day is the evil thereof and we should not carry over into tomorrow the bad financial decisions made today or struggle with debts made yesterday. **We must not encumber the future for present convenience.** Credit is the means to live beyond your income and must be taken seriously. As a good steward of financial resources for family and faith, believers must make mature decisions with the best interest of spouse, children, the kingdom and a personal legacy. We must follow the rules of kingdom stewardship or suffer the spiritual and personal consequences of failure. Scripture discourages debt *"The rich rule over the poor and the borrower is servant to the lender."* (Proverbs 22:7) In the context of debt, always thank of the impact on family, legacy, and kingdom outreach.

God gives the Power to get Wealth

Abraham and others in the Old Testament were wealthy in livestock and in silver and gold. The possession of wealth is not regarded as bad, but, on the contrary, prosperity is a sign of the blessing of God. Individuals become wealthy to advance God's agenda not for personal use. Gifts from the wealthy may be an act of worship as one returns goods and services for kingdom use. Nicodemus, Joseph of Arimathea, and Zacchaeus were men of means in the New Testament. It may be inferred from the Gospel records that James and John were enriched by their fishing business. All these men were use of God for good. Wealth may be the result of industry and poverty the result of idleness or slack hands (Proverbs 10:4), or the result of the special blessing of God. There is a warning (Deuteronomy 8:17, 18) to be careful not to claim, *"My power and the might of my hand has made me wealthy, but remember God gave the power to get wealth."*

There are some liabilities to wealth when one does not clearly understand what God has entrusted them with affluence. Those possessing wealth are open to certain kinds of offenses against which scripture frequently warns; such as:

High-Mindedness

Warn those who are rich in this present world not to think highly of themselves, not to trust in uncertain riches, but in the living God, who bestows on us all that we richly enjoy; 18. let them enrich their lives with charitable deeds, always ready to contribute and share with the fellowship; 19. some have laid up the foundation of a good treasure against the world to come that they may grasp true life eternal.
(1 Timothy 6:17 EDNT)

Oppression of the Poor

5. I command you to listen, my cherished band of believers, were not the poor of this world chosen to be rich in faith, and heirs of the kingdom promised to all who love God? 6. But you have dishonored the poor man. Do not rich men dominate you, and drag you before the law-courts? 7. Do they not blaspheme that worthy name by which you are called? 8. If you keep the noble law according to the scripture, you should unselfishly love your neighbor as yourself. 9. But if you flatter the great, you bring upon yourself guilt, and the law reckons you a transgressor. 10. For the man who fails at one point, but keeps the balance of the law, is liable for all the penalties. (James 2:5-10 EDNT)

Selfishness

Be on guard against greed: for a man's life is not based on wealth or possessions. (Luke 12:15 and 16)

Dishonesty

9. And I say to you, Make friends for yourselves by the wise use of money, so when the money is gone your friends will receive you. 10. He who is faithful in small things is trustworthy in big things. 11. If you have not been faithful in the wealth of this world, who will trust you with true riches? 12. And if you have not been faithful with another man's wealth, who shall give you personal possessions? 13. No steward can serve two masters: he will hate one and love the other or attach himself to one and detest the other. You cannot serve both God and the false god of wealth.
(Luke 19:9-13 EDNT)

Self-Importance

[11] *The rich have an excessively favorable opinion of themselves;* but *the poor discerns their self-importance.* [12] *When the righteous triumph, there is*

celebration; but when the wicked rise to power, people hide for fear. (Proverbs 28:11-12 EDOT)

Self-Reliance

[11] The rich man's wealth is his protected city, with walls too high for others to climb. (Proverbs 18:11 EDOT)

No Guidance on Financial Matters

It is of interest that the New Testament use of "lucre" to indicate money or profit refers four of the five places to the income of ministers. This strongly suggests that those in leadership roles were susceptible to the bad influences and power of money. Sadly, this trend continues in the present day to the shame of Christianity. When leaders fail to understand the proper use money, there will be no instruction for the congregation in kingdom economics and the acquisition and use of personal wealth. How can there be teaching with enthusiasm about *"money matters,"* when leaders either do not understand or refuse to follow known scriptural truths.

Congregations not Well-served

In many cases, the congregation is not well-served and has been short-changed. The word *enthusiasm* is based on the Greek root *"enthro"* meaning *"God in you."* When God is not a part of a leader's concept and construct of money matters, there will be no excitement in guiding the congregation on the subject. No wonder some congregations are strapped for funds. It is easy to understand Paul on this matter. He was a self-employed tent maker who earned his own keep and also financially supported his own ministry team. Yet he wrote Timothy about leaders who served well, *Let the seniors who practice oversight well be counted worthy of two-fold money, **especially those who labor preaching and teaching.*** (1 Timothy 5:17 EDNT)

Then there is the case of Peter with no pocket money on his way to pray and encountered a need: 6. And Peter said, **I have no silver or gold, but I will give you what I do have: In the name of Jesus Christ of Nazareth stand up and walk.** 7. Taking his right hand, Peter lifted him up: and instantly his feet and ankle bones became strong. (Acts 3:1-7 EDNT) That is powerful ministry service freely given to someone in need. Note Paul's words to young Timothy:

> *5.You know that we never used the language of flattery, and God knows **we never attempted to enrich ourselves***: *6. for we never sought praise from you or others, when we might have been burdensome to you as apostles of Christ. 7. But we were tender among you, even as a nursing mother warmly takes pleasure in her children: 8. so affectionately longing for you, we were willing to share with you, not only the gospel of God, but also well-pleased to share our lives, because you were valued by us. 9. You **remember our long and hard labor night and day, because we would not burden you for expenses, but freely preached the gospel of God unto you.** 10. You are witnesses and so is God, how upright, honest and blameless was our conduct among you that believe:* (1 Timothy 2:5-10 EDNT)

Appreciating Personal Wealth

When one fully appreciates the value and use of wealth, they are moving into closer fellowship with God and mankind. The valuing of God's blessings is the first step in developing whole life behavior as a steward. Systemic failures in financial stability for family and faith-based entities, may well be attributed to poor stewardship of the resources already provided by God. Believers must develop an appreciation for personal wealth.

Be Good Stewards of Grace

7. The end of all things is near: live wisely, and keep your senses awake to greet the times of prayer. 8. Above all embrace each other in love that is constant and intense: because love covers a multitude of sins. 9. Never begrudge the hospitality you show one another. **10. As each has received a gift from God, so let all use such gifts in the service of one another, as good stewards of God's multisided grace.** *11. Should any man speak, let him speak words sent from God; if a man serves, let him do it with God-given ability: that God may be glorified in all things through Jesus Christ, to whom be praise and dominion for ever and ever. Amen.*
(1 Peter 4:7-11 EDNT)

VI

Appreciating
Personal Wealth

7. For we brought nothing into this world, neither can we carry out anything. 8. Let us be content with food and clothing. 9. <u>*But those who are determined to be rich are tempted and caught in a trap, and into many senseless and dangerous appetites, such desires cause men to sink into present destruction and later punishment in hell.*</u> *10. For* **the root of all evil is the love of money: while some craving money have wandered away from the faith and suffered many self-inflicted and discouraging sorrows.** (1 Timothy 6:7-10 EDNT)

The Starting Place

Wealth creation is not the starting place: the divine plan is to start a family and invest in a home place. The hearth of the "old home place" becomes an altar of memories and answered prayers. All earned income is stipulated for family living and legacy, but all over what is necessary and reasonable becomes *"wealth – more than enough"* and is designated funds to regularly share in giving, based on personal and family ability. When one follows God's Plan, regardless of their financial position, valuable treasure is stored in Heaven's Bank and is available for Kingdom use. It is Kingdom Wealth rather than earthly affluence that counts. However, true prosperity is to consider the "value" of personal funds from God's viewpoint, not by a monetary or budgetary consideration. True wealth for participants in the Kingdom is their "purchasing power" based on divine evaluation of existing funds. For example: if the widow's mite had a higher *"coinage value"* in the eyes of Jesus than all the other gifts of the rich, then Kingdom Wealth should have more "purchasing power" for things needed to advance the family and kingdom endeavors. Believers share based on their ability and God multiplies their gifts to meet the needs of the Kingdom. Obedience and the willing sacrifice of believers builds wealth to advance the Kingdom of God!

Economics and Personal Wealth

Secular economics defines wealth in contrast to the Old and New Testaments. Wealth defined by secular authorities is the accumulation and comfort of material things. The Biblical definition considers everything good that God has provided as personal wealth: friends, family, children, food, shelter, work, even a stable government. This includes salvation, fellowship with believers, blessings from worship, and a missional lifestyle of witness. Personal wealth is literally all the good things that God provides and entrust to believers.

17. Warn them who are rich in this present world not to think highly of themselves, not to trust in uncertain riches, but in **the living God, who bestows on us all** *that we richly enjoy;* *18. let them enrich their lives with charitable deeds, always ready to contribute and share with the fellowship; 19. some have laid up the foundation of a good treasure against the world to come that they may grasp true life eternal.* (1 Timothy 6:17-19 EDNT)

Money has various Meanings

Since early civilization money, in any form, has exerted great influence on mankind. According to my son, Barton, *"Wealth magnifies character--Who you are without money multiplies with each added dollar."* The variety of meanings demonstrates the different perspective on money and its use. φιλάργυρος (*philarguros*) -- meaning: riches, loving money, possessions. μαμμωνᾶς (*mamónas*) meaning: riches, money, possessions. νόμισμα was the ancient Greek word for "money" and is derived from *nomos* (νόμος) "anything assigned, a usage, custom, law, ordinance." It appears impossible to be a True Servant of God and simultaneously be a slave to **money.** The Greek had a meaning that does not translate well into English: "Money had a meaning 'to need' and 'to use together." Aramaic, viewed money as riches, possessions, property and wealth.

Where is the Storehouse?

In Malachi 3, Jews were encouraged, even in the time of a weak harvest, to bring the "full tithe" or 10% of the crop to the "storehouse" which was a place to store grain in the temple. This was designed to support the Levites as caretakers of the tabernacle. This principle in the New Testament is to give voluntarily to support the needs of others, Christian workers and expand Christian outreach.

Support the Needs of Others

All who believed kept together, and all their possessions were shared; 45. Goods and property were sold and distributed as every man had need. 46. And they agreed to meet daily in the temple and to break bread from house to house, and they took meals cheerfully and with personal commitment. 47. Praising God and having favor with all the people. And the Lord added to the church daily those being saved. (Acts 2:45-47 EDNT).

*24. when I travel to Spain, I will visit you: for I hope to include you in my journey and be aided forward after I have enjoyed your company for a while. 25. But first I must go to Jerusalem to deliver a collection to the saints. 26. For the provinces of Macedonia and Achaia have freely made a contribution for the poor saints in Jerusalem. 27. **It was a pleasure for the Gentiles, being debtors and partakers of spiritual things, to feel responsible to minister in material things.** 28. When I have finished this task and assured the delivery of the collection, I plan to visit you on my way to Spain. (Romans 15:24-28 EDNT)*

Support Christian Workers

7. Does a soldier ever go to war at his own expense? Who plants a vineyard and does not eat of the fruit? Or who feeds a flock and does not taste the milk? 8. Do I speak as a man; does not the law say the same thing? 9. For it is written in Moses' law; You shall not muzzle the ox that treads out the corn. Does God take care of oxen? 10. Does He not speak assuredly these words for us? No doubt for us was this written: that he who plows should plow in hope; and he who

threshes in hope should be partaker of his hope.
*11. **If we have sown to you spiritual seeds, is it a great thing that we should reap some material benefits?** 12. If others have authority over you, do we not have greater rights? Nevertheless, we have not exercised this power; but endured all things, lest we should hinder the gospel of Christ. 13. You know that those who serve in the temple take their food from the temple. And those who attend regularly at the altar share in the sacrificial offerings. 14. In the same way the Lord has commanded that they who preach the gospel should live of the gospel.* (1 Corinthians 9:7-14 EDNT)

*17. Let the seniors who practice oversight well be counted worthy of twofold money, especially those who labor preaching and teaching. 18. For scripture says, **You shall not muzzle the ox treading out the corn. And, the laborer is worthy of his compensatio**n.* (1 Timothy 5:17-18 EDNT)

Expand Christian Outreach

*10. But I rejoiced greatly in the Lord that at last your care of me has flourished again; wherein you were also concerned but lacked opportunity. 11. Not that I speak in regard to need: **for I have learned, in whatever circumstance I am, therewith to be self-sufficient**. 12. I understand how to deal with humble circumstances, and I know how to have more than enough: everywhere and in all things, I have learned to be well-fed and to be hungry, both to have plenty and to suffer need. 13. I can do all things through Christ who provides me strength. 14. Notwithstanding my circumstance, you have done well in contributing your share toward my hardship. 15. You Philippians know that in the beginning of the gospel, when I departed for Macedonia, no church but you, shared* *with me concerning financial matters. 16. For even in Thessalonica you sent funds twice to provide for my needs. 17. **It was not a desire for financial gifts: but I desired that a harvest may abound to your account.** 18. <u>But I have more than enough; my needs are fully satisfied, having received of Epaphroditus the gifts you sent, they were like a sweet-smelling sacrifice acceptable and well pleasing to God. 19. But my God shall supply all your needs according to the wealth of His glory by Christ Jesus.</u> (*Philippians 4:15-16 EDNT)

Needs of Christian Work and Ministry

While a tithe is a good standard to use for giving; it is clear the early church did not focus on a specific amount but rather on meeting the needs of others.   In fact, the New Testament believers gave much more to meet the growing needs of Christian outreach and ministry.

*1. Now concerning the gathering of **funds for the saints**, follow the directions I gave to the congregations of Galatia. 2<u>. On the first day of each week remember how God has prospered you and put aside your gifts in a safe place</u>, so no collections will be necessary when I come. 3. When I arrive whomever you approved by letters, I will send with your freewill gifts to Jerusalem. 4. And if it is advantageous that I go, they shall go with me. 5. I plan to pass through Macedonia and I will visit you when I do. 6. And it may be that I will remain with you through the winter, that you may assist me on the next phase of my journey.* (1 Corinthians 16:1-12 EDNT).

Kingdom Economics

God intended that faith-based entities be supported and sustained by the moral and material interest of individual believers. God provides individuals with access to funds, and out of these Provisions of Providence, believers deposit into resources that advance Kingdom interests. The tithe is based on total earnings, but a gift is valued in terms of the giver. The widow's mite was measured by what she had left. Jesus assessed the gift of the widow as more valuable to the Kingdom than all the symbolic gifts of the wealthy because their gifts cost them almost nothing. All faith-based entities must see the small gifts of the poor as they are "valued by Jesus" and realize the purchase power of such gifts are not measured in secular monetary terms but by Kingdom value to the beneficiary. This is the way Kingdom economics work. Gifts from the heart have an added "coinage value" based on divine evaluation of what the gift cost the giver.

Believers Create Wealth for the Kingdom

Paul counseled the Corinthians to *"abound in the grace of liberality."* His example was the poor Macedonians who first gave themselves to God and then out of their deep poverty gave liberally to support the Gospel outreach. Consider the Scriptural method of giving: *without show* (Matthew 6:3); *regularly in proportion to personal assets* (1 Corinthians 16:2); *and liberally and cheerfully* (2 Corinthians 9:7). Believers should use these guidelines to advance the kingdom.

Use of Kingdom Wealth

Faith-based leaders must be wise in the purchase of equipment and services. Unless they understand that their account stored in Heaven's Bank is for the advancement of the Gospel, they will normally spend more than is needed for things that do not advance the Kingdom of God. When leaders calculate purchasing power only on the numerical value of coinage without considering the divinely added "wealth factor" based on the "sweat equity" of the giver and the divine multiplication of the "coinage value," they waste Kingdom resources.

Energy Exchange

Voluntary labor for the Kingdom is an asset of value for a faith-based entity. All believers are in "full-time" Christian service regardless of how they earn their "living." The faith-based lifestyle and service to God is not about money; it is about a personal connection with God and a sincere relationship with others. Spiritual service is not determined by how or how much one earns, but depends on their relationship with God and their concern for others. Christian workers are provided a stipend to be free to follow God's Call. When faith-based groups make service to God and outreach to the lost about money, they fail to understand the wealth stored in the Bank of Heaven that comes from the gifts of the poor: outreach is not about money; it is about spiritual obedience and caring for the needs of others! Energy is exchanged for coinage. If one has money, labor can be purchased to do the work. If one has no funds, they must exchange their energy (labor) for "enough income" to support their family and to do their share to advance the Good News of Grace. Little is much in God's sight!

When Did Men Start Praying

The first parents, Adam and Eve, failed to pass on all the knowledge learned from their daily walk with God in the Garden after they became exposed to Satan and sin. The shed blood of an animal provided clothing for Adam and Eve. *"Without the shedding of blood there was no remission"* was made obvious by the way God dealt with changes in the behavior of Adam and Eve.

Sacrifice and the sheading of blood became an obvious tenant of faith. Cain and Abel knew that the worship of God required a sacrifice, but was not clear on the "issue of blood." Cain's bloodless offering was rejected, but Abel's lamb was accepted.

This further validated God's strategy for forgiveness and parents obligation to share knowledge about their relationship with God. A failure at this level, resulted in the first murder in the human race. God gave Adam a replacement for Abel, his name was Seth, meaning "anointed or compensation." When Seth had a son, Adam's first grandson, Genesis 4:26 *"Then men began to call on the name of the Lord!"* The first grandchild prompted the need for prayer. It was a family need that initiated family prayer. What happened to the family altar, the family pew, the family table where God shared His blessings?

A Mother's Packed Lunch

The lunch of a little boy was *"enough and then some"* for Jesus to feed 5,000 and have twelve baskets full left over. There were no banquet table or special seats. The Children's Bread was spread on the ground for the hungry followers of Jesus. This was spiritual multiplication of a mother's effort. Can you imagine the knowledge and respect gained by a small boy when his mother's preparation was used so greatly by the Lord. Why do parents fail to take the little they have and let God multiply it to sufficient levels to meet the needs of those around us? Perhaps the Deacons should be more serious about the Prayers before and after the Offering. All giving should be a thanksgiving offering to God and a teaching experience for others about Kingdom work. Did you ever wonder when, where, and why people begin giving offering to God? Why do we give offerings during worship? Here are some suggested reasons. Perhaps you can add others.

- Do not come into the presence of God empty-handed.
- Do no give to God what costs you nothing.
- Give of our best to the Lord not the least;
- Give the first fruits of your labor and not the dregs.
- An offering is an act of faith in God and the future.
- Offerings must be given in faith to be blessed.
- God looks at the heart as well as what is in the hand.

- Giving gifts to the Kingdom is part of maintaining a "present tense" relationship with God.

*23. **Therefore if you bring your gift to the altar and remember that your brother has a grievance against you; 24. leave your gift before the altar, and first make peace with your brother and then return and offer your gift.*** (Matthew 5:23-24 EDNT)

In addition to the process of reconciling with others who may have something against you, there are other spiritual things in which believers participate to remain current in their fellowship with God:

1. Celebration –of our position in Christ, acknowledge Divine leadership (1 Corinthians 12:26-33)

2. Collect –bring together, bring or pull together –short prayer including collecting into one the needs of the congregation, a petition for one thing in order that lifestyle is improved, (Acts 2:1-13; Mark 12:28-34; Matthew 12:4-30; 18:20)

3. Confession – acknowledgment, profession, assertion (1 John 1:5-10)

4. Communion –unity, closeness, intimacy– The Eucharis is "gratitude, thanksgiving." Lord's Super, worship, spiritual union. (1 Corinthians 11:17-34)

5. Consensus –agreement, accord, harmony, unanimity, (Acts 15:22-29)

6. Commission—directive, instruction, charge, guidance – (Mark 16:9 -20]

7. Contribution ---gifts based on individual and family ability to support Kingdom work. This includes a moral and ethical lifestyle.

8. Conduct –organized course of personal behavior plus demeanor=appearance and behavior, the way others see you that includes reconciliation before bringing gifts to the altar.

What is in your Lunch Basket?

Line up under God's arrangements with what you have whether it is a penny or a pound, a gift or a talent, a song or poem; an essay or a book. After your kingdom offering, God can use what remains for family support and regularly shared portion of income to supply the needs of the poor and faith-based workers. This is a hard lesson to learn, but a most valued lesson in the field of individual achievement, personal wealth and funding of faith-based endeavors. The Mother who prepared lunch for her son had provided "more than enough" for his lunch and "then some" which provided Jesus with the basis for expansion and to feed many others. A good mother thinks about contingencies. What might my son need today? What do you pack for your children? What is in your "lunch box?" What is in the lunch basket?

Cattle of a 1,000 Hills

An old story about an individual short of funds was told to talk to God about the matter. Draw on your account in the Bank of Heaven and God may use a branch office near you. When you have more month than money, remember that God owns the cattle of 1,000 hills and the gold in the hills! We must all permit God to guide our financial planning and the spiritual choices to share with others. This old proverb remains true, *"Opportunity equals obligation!"*

Raising the Annual Mission Offering

There is a story told to me my by maternal grandfather of a rural congregation desiring to raise funds for a missionary endeavor. They asked each farmer to select a calf and raise it for market. The full sale price was to be given for missions. One farmer looked over his herd and selected a weak little calf for the missionary drive. But when it came market time, the weakling had developed into a prize bull which the farmer decided to keep. He contrived a story that the calf was sold for a small amount. Running late on the Sunday he was to give the price of the calf, as he arrived the choir was singing **"The Half has never been told!"**

You guessed it: the farmer heard different words: to him they were singing **"the calf has never been sold!"** He rushed home to get the full market value of the prize bull and returned to confess to his selfish plan. Perhaps he had read Acts 5 about the deceit of Ananias and Sapphira when they kept back part of the price of the land promised for the Apostles' fund-raising effort for the poor.

1. Come you rich men, bemoan yourselves and cry over the miseries that are coming upon you. 2. Corruption has fallen on your wealth and your fine clothes are food for moths. 3. Your gold and silver are corroded and poisoned by rust; and the decay is proof to you of how worthless your coins are. It is a canker which will eat into your very flesh like fire. These are your final days and you spent them storing up a personal destiny of retribution. 4. You have kept back the pay of the reapers who worked your land, and the

*great number of men in the Lord's army has heard
their cries against you. God listened to their complaint.
5. You feasted on earth, your heart was comforted
with luxuries but this day dooms you to slaughter.*
(James 5:1-12 EDNT)

Always Pray about Your Participation

Just as I was introduced to speak at a Black
convention in Jacksonville, Florida, during a time
of civil rights stress, an usher lady dressed in white
came running down the aisle. She was speaking
loudly *"Don't murder anybody, God said don't kill
anybody."* Being the only white person present, I
kept the pulpit between us. As she continued to
voice her concern, she put her hand into a brown
paper bag and began to pull out something. Then
she continued, *"My daughter wanted to come to this
convention, but she didn't have any shoes. So, we
prayed..."* Then she pulled out a sandal with dog teeth
marks on it and began to show it to the congregation.
*"My dog Rusty done drug in this shoe, but my
daughter couldn't come to this meeting with one shoe,
so we* prayed again." Pulling the mate to the sandal
out of the paper bag, she began to rejoice about
Rusty finding the other sandal.

After a few moments of rejoicing by the
congregation about a prayer answering dog, one
deacon stood up and said, "If Rusty, ever has any
pups, I want one! Then the Pastor asked, *"May I
borrow Rusty for a few days; we never know exactly
how God will answer our prayers!"*

VII

Focusing
Light On The Family

Appreciating Value

There are two things that appreciate in value
over time: property and people. Investing in property
is a risk, but overtime it normally increases in value.
On the other hand, the surest increase in value
is an investment in people. The "value added" is
something that can be seen from the beginning and
throughout life. Children are an asset that grows
daily and increases in value. Friends come next,
they are better than money in the bank, because one
can utilize the interest of friendship without depleting
the principle value. Building friendships is a central
aspect of growing personal wealth.

An Old Custom

An Old Testament custom among Hebrew
families was for the father of the prospective groom
to go to the father of the bride to be and make
arrangements for the marriage. Then the groom was
to live at his father's house and spend12 months
preparing a place for his bride. After the wedding
according to the Ceremonial Law: *"If a man has
recently married, he must not be sent to war or have*

any other duty laid on him. For one year he is to be free to stay at home and bring happiness to the wife he has married." (Deuteronomy 24:5 NIV)

A Newer Model

In an early effort to learn about the sociology of selecting a mate, a process no longer the prevailing fashion in Jamaica was discovered. In the 1950's a Jamaican cultural model of a non-dating, objective mate-selection plan was used in some faith-based circles rather than the current subjective courtship and personal dating process. This model usually controlled by the church led to a **brokered marriage_ proposal_**articulated by the local clergy representing the potential bridegroom. It appeared to be an excellent way for a young man to find a moral mate and begin a mature marriage relationship with the blessing of the church and the bride's family.

A Degraded System

In a follow-up study five decades later, romantic love and serial dating had replaced most of the working arrangements that for generations brought couples together with the mature guidance of parents which enabled them to launch a stable marriage relationship in which they could build a family. This degraded system is now the common model and is part of the antecedent cause for the incompatibility in marriage which leads to scarcity and a financial deficit and limited parenting for children, a lack of concern for the poor, and little or no support for religious or kingdom enterprises.

A Worthy and Compatible Spouse

How should the process begin? A first step to a stable family is finding a worthy and compatible spouse. Learning to live with this person is a harder task. The goal is a peaceable household where children and parents can be nourished in the *"Faith once delivered to the Saints"* and enjoy a seat at the Lord's Table with access to the Children's Bread.

> *Do not be yoked together with unbelievers. For what do righteousness and wickedness have in common? Or what fellowship can light have with darkness? (2 Corinthians 6:14) [or do not mate or marry unsuitably/ incorrectly or come under a different yoke inconsistent with your faith. Be angry at the transgression of divine law-- (**immorality, injustice, sinful behavior**) Yet do not sin. Do not let the sun go down on your wrath.* (Ephesians 4:26 EDNT)

It is clear from Psalms 127 that *"children are a heritage of the Lord: and the fruit of the womb is a reward from the wife. Children are like arrows of a might man and happy is the man who has his quiver full of children, because they are his heritage"* (*a comfort, an inheritance, a future*). Marriage and family are the perfect beginning of wealth. Good planning, budgeting, and careful spending habits are the means to increase family resources to leave a legacy to children and grandchildren and have available funds to care for others and support humanitarian and kingdom activities.

A Stable Family

Notwithstanding, the value-added elements received from regularly family participation in religious programs/activities including scheduled worship services; it should be accepted that churches do not make good families: it is good and stable families that make good places of worship. There must be genuine conversion, the consistent following of Jesus, fidelity in marriage, and honest relationship with the secular society to create a stable family that will benefit the local places of worship and kingdom initiatives.

Good and Strong Men

The pristine congregation in Jerusalem selected, as the first deacon, good and strong men with stable families to assist with special needs in the congregation. (Acts 6:1-6) Enduring families led by good men of honest report, who walked in spiritual fellowship with the Lord, were chosen and appointed to take care of cerain2 business to free senior leadership for times of prayer and ministry of the Word. Those men and their families had significant influence on the congregation. When the family's heart and soul is in the work of God, they will assist in caring for the saints, win souls, demonstrate concern for the poor, and follow the guidance for pure religion stated in James 1:27, and freely support the financial needs of kingdom endeavors.

The Cause of Scarcity

The difficulty in faith-based finance can normally be traced to less than a missional mindset in the family particularly to the use of money. The problem is normally a lack of regular and proportional support for the kingdom, not the scarcity of funds. Little is much in the Hand of God. Provided leadership in the church and the family firmly understood and practice the scriptural principles of economics and personal wealth there would be sufficient funds for the family, even a surplus for a legacy and support for faith-based endeavors.

What is the Coinage Value?

Wealth is not the visible coinage value of money; it is the value added by God based on sweat equity and proper use of funds that creates sufficient support for the family, even more than enough if used wisely, with an overage to assist others and meet legitimate kingdom need. The intention with which a gift is given determines the spiritual coinage value. All gifts are measured by the personal sweat equity in the gift or a measure of the actual physical labor that earned or created the gift. Have we forgotten the two small coins of the widow that Jesus judged the coinage value to be more than all the contributions of the wealthy? Do we remember the little boy's lunch of bread and fish that Jesus expanded to feed several thousand with twelve baskets left over? Why only twelve baskets left over? Perhaps the disciples only had twelve baskets available.

Scarcity of Baskets

A Sunday school teacher asked, *"Why were only 12 baskets full left over?"* A small boy quickly replied," *Maybe it was only 12 disciples with just 12 baskets. Had there been more disciples and more baskets there would have been more fish and bread.*" Can we no longer trust God to enable us to gather enough "daily bread" to care for the family with some left over? Where are the extra baskets to carry the overage to others? Wealth means to have "more than enough" in order to assist others and initiate new approaches to advancing the kingdom by supporting faith-based operations. When God's provisions are misused, scarcity occurs for all concerned. This does not have to happen!

The Giver is Twice Blessed

God requires that the family be adequately supported and equates failure to accomplish this support worse than being an agnostic. Then comes responsible places of worship and faithful workers in kingdom endeavors, and in this process the poor cannot be neglected. To neglect the less fortunate is to miss the greater blessing spoken of by Jesus, "***It is more blessed to give than to receive.***" When believers have more than enough they can assist others. To be adequately blessed is to supply enough for a larger blessing in giving. Of course, the needy are blessed by the assistance of others, but the giver is doubly blessed. This is a little understood spiritual dynamics at work! Yet, the receiver still has concerns: where is the next meal, what about the rent, utilities, etc. Gifts to the poor only solve the immediate problem. The giver must assist with their tomorrows.

Sound advice about work and planning is also a valuable gift.

Where God Guides, He Provides

The premise of this book is that faith-based ventures do not have financial problems; they normally have dysfunctional relationship at the family level or are operating outside the preferred will of God. It is good and stable families that normally support God's work. When couples and their children walk together on the pathway designed for believers, the family has sufficient for themselves and enough left over to support kingdom efforts. Where God guides, He provides! A valuable insight comes from the book Giving 2.0 by Laura Arrillaga-Andreessen. Her position on being a philanthropist *"is anyone who gives anything –time, money, experience, skills, and networks--in any amount to create a better world."* The widows two coins made her a blessed philanthropist in the eyes of Jesus. It is not the amount; it is the cost to the giver that adds coinage value to giving. The Creator God who made the world and everything in it, surely can multiply both the gifts and service offered in faith to make the world a better place. What can you do…what will you do??

Chief End of God

There is a story of children studying the Westminster Shorter Catechism and came to this question:

"Q. What is the chief end of man?

A. Man's chief end is to glorify God and to enjoy him forever."

A young girl was asked to repeat the precept and then the teacher asked, *"What then is the chief end of God?"* The girl answered, **"Since the chief end of man is to glorify God and to enjoy him forever; then the chief end of God must be to glorify man and enjoy him forever."** Out of the mouth of a child came the wisdom of the ages! God desires the praise, worship, and fellowship of His creation. Mankind is to glorify God and enjoy Him forever! When will we learn that God speaks through innocence and obedience.

The Garden Walk

Adam was made from the dust of the earth and placed in a gorgeous garden with a helpmate to enjoy God's provided bounty. They walked with God in the cool of the day in the garden. This walk fulfilled God's reason for the existence of man. They were made to glorify God and enjoy Him forever. Man, had easy work in beautiful surroundings naming the animals and plants and must have looked forward to their daily walk with God. The Creator intended man and his family to live in a good and safe surroundings, but Satan soon interfered with this Master Family Plan. Paradise was lost, and the first family was thrust out into the harsh reality of a cruel world and forced to work under difficult circumstances for their daily bread.

Limited Understanding of Worship

Satan was unrelenting in efforts to hinder the Plan of God by providing partial truth which hindered the understanding of the children concerning worship and redemption. Satan continued to fight against a stable family by meddling with the way the brothers offered themselves and their proceeds in worship to God. The sons of Adam and Eve learned that God expected them to earn their bread by the sweat and toil of hard work.   Cain offered a vegetarian offering from his crop for worship while Abel provided a lamb as a blood sacrifice from his flock. Both offered the fruit of their labor, but their understanding was limited: "without the shedding of blood, there is no remission of sin."

Good vs. Evil

This division brought bitterness and resentment into the family resulting in the loss of respect for human life and closed the door on family values. Sadly, the battle between good and evil continued throughout the Old Testament, spilled over into the New Testament congregations and the half-truth of the Serpent continues to influence the present-day faith-based groups. Centuries later congregations still have a dichotomy in worship; some see the "worth-ship" of God in their worship service while others entertain and promote "go and do" programs without adding the spiritual dimension of a missional lifestyle to the congregants. This form of godliness without the Power of the Spirit continues the battle for the family and spiritual warfare rages inside and outside the sacred walls of places of worship. In this struggle, the promise of good news and great joy for all God's people is lost and the *"peace and good will"* that attended the praising of God at the birth of Jesus has been smothered by sectarian and family squabbles. The battle of good vs. evil continues.

Treasure vs. Heart

People are divided into weekly training groups to continue sectarian conflicts and little is accomplished to heal the wounds or strengthen the daily lifestyle of churchgoers. Few are truly glorifying God, and most have just enough religion to make them and their family miserable. This does not support God's plan for a wholesome family life and when the heart is not committed to true worship the financial resources to support the family, the less fortunate and kingdom work suffers. Scripture declared *"Where the treasure is there will the heart be also."* However, the converse is also true "**Where the heart is there the treasure will also be.**"

> *5. Then the Pharisees and scribes asked Jesus, Why do your disciples not walk according to the tradition of the elders, but eat bread with unwashed hands? 6. He answered, you hypocrites, Isaiah prophesied and described you,* **This people honors me with their lips, but their heart is far from me. 7. Their worship is empty, teaching for doctrines the precepts of men. 8. You give up what God commanded and cling to the tradition of men,** *as the washing of pots and cups, 9. and He said to them,* **Full well you reject the commandments of God, that you may keep your own tradition.** *(Mark 7:5-9 EDNT)*

Focused on Family Division

Making a judgment is the ability to make decisions or come to conclusions based on known facts. Jesus used His wisdom to construct an oxymoron to emphasize the purpose of His ministry, *"You suppose that I came to bring **peace**, I tell you, not so, but rather **division**."* An oxymoron is when two contradictory words come together in one phrase, so **peace/division** are two contradictory words pushed together and are considered to be a self-contradiction. Jesus also said, *"I came to set the world on fire"* and *"I wish it were already started."* In the biblical sense, **fire means light** which came from a candle, a lamp, a torch, or a fire. It appears that since the family is designed as a unit, **family/division** may also be an oxymoron. Jesus said clearly, He came to bring division to the family by shining the Light of His Presence on difficulties which divide the family and hinder kingdom growth.

In mathematics, the easiest way to solve a problem is to divide it into parts. Problems addressed in this passage may be solved by "moral algebra;" that is, breaking the situation apart and considering both the antecedent cause and the solution.

> *49. I came to set the world on fire; and I wish it were already started. 50. But I have an engagement and I am impatient until it is accomplished!* **51.** *You suppose that I came to bring **peace**, I tell you, not so, but rather **division**: 52. Henceforth, **a family of five will be divided in one house, three against two, and two against three**. 53. A father will decide one way about Me and the son another; the mother will be set against*

the daughter, and the daughter against the mother;
and the mother-in-law will oppose the daughter-in-law,
and the daughter-in-law will be at variance with the
mother-in-law. (Luke 12:49-53 EDNT)

Moral Algebra

The word "algebra" means the *"reunion of*
broken parts" and is the study of rules of operations,
relations, and the constructions and concepts
informed by these rules. A kind of moral algebra is
a construct that can enhance an ethical lifestyle of
a family, because algebra is a process where one
learns to solve problems by observing the parts. The
rules and guidance in Scripture relative to family life
are similar to a moral dilemma. There is an algebraic
concept in the moral practice of a faith-based family.
Basic algebra lessons emphasize the practice or
action of understanding the question and intelligently
and simply arriving at an answer. Just as students
dislike the study of elementary algebra, troubled
families are normally reluctant to study the rules and
regulations of faith-based behavior that could solve
their problems and open the windows of heaven.

The Immature Want an Easy Way

It appears that the immature always wants an
easy way and are not willing to learn the rules that
make life work for the good of all. The *"reunion*
of broken parts" and the study of moral rules of
operations and relationships, and the constructions
and concepts informed by these rules are part of
God's design. Faith-based experience can put the
broken parts of family life together and once these

parts are understood and working, a moral lifestyle that enhances family life and benefits the local place of worship, will be demonstrated for all to observe.

Examining Lifestyle Regularly

Scripture is clear, *"We cannot live by bread alone;"* there is a clear need for the nourishment of the Word of God. The Word is a measuring stick to determine the quality of family life and the true value of worship. Believers must check their moral compass daily to determine the path they are to follow. The stepping stones of sacred writings clearly mark the true path: either the pathway leads upward toward a positive future or downward toward the valley of despair? Listen to your heart; it speaks with a strong voice. Understanding the motives that guide daily living is an important check on the quality of family life. Is your faith-based behavior adequately supporting your witness to family and friends? Is your heart committed to the Messiah's message and to your spouse? If so, when two agree they can walk together toward stated goals. Remember, long-term goals are to keep you from becoming discouraged with short-term failures. Fixing family problems is not an easy process: God, family and friends are ready to assist any positive move toward a more stable family.

Focus on Family Life

The way one behaves in the family environment sends a message to both family and friends about personal health and the spiritual status of the family. Poor judgment causes bad decisions and one becomes a *"good bad example"* to others. Losing your temper in a difficult situation speaks to a lack of maturity to handle the normal stress of daily life. An instance of a spilled glass of milk illustrates that a problem provides an opportunity to demonstrate mature behavior. It seems a young grandchild spilled his milk and those present waited to see the reaction of the quick-spoken grandfather. The grandfather simply knelt down, put his arm around the child and begin cleaning up the mess: but the words were more meaningful than his action. He said to the child, *"When I was a little boy I used to spill my milk, too. I'll get you some more!"* This was a great comfort to the child and a good example of moral and ethical behavior to those present. Others are always watching and listening; especially the children and the critics.

How is your Albedo?

Albedo literally means white and technically it is the rate of reflected light from a surface based on the total light falling upon that surface. For example, the earth's moon has no light of its own. What is seen is the reflected light, the *albedo*, of the sunlight as it is thrown back or returned toward the sun. That is what is seen from the earth. The moon absorbs much of the light and only a small part is reflected back into the atmosphere. Are you reflecting light to others? How is your spiritual *albedo?* Light is the absence of darkness. *Are you reflecting the Light of the Universe to the darkness of the world? Can two walk together without agreeing on the direction?* (Amos 3:3).

5. This then is the message which we have heard of Him, and announce to you, that God is light, and no darkness can find a place in Him. 6. If we say that we have fellowship with Him, and at the same time walk in darkness, we lie, and are not living the truth: 7. but if we walk in the light, as He is in the light, we have fellowship one with another, and the blood of Jesus Christ His Son cleanses us from all sin. (1 John 1:5-7 EDNT)

Moral Darkness

Division in the family brings moral darkness to the household and the neighborhood. ***"Take care that the reflected light in you does not come from moral darkness."*** How is your Albedo? Are you reflecting the light from your association with Jesus? Reflected light is called *albedo.* The moon has reflected light from the sun. Believers are to let their light shine by receiving spiritual light from the Son of God, absorbing some and reflecting the rest to others. You have a choice: you can be "good" or a "good bad example."

*33. No man who lights a lamp puts it in a closet, nor under a box, but on a lamp, stand so all may see the light. 34. The lamp of the body is the eye: therefore, when your eye is focused your whole body has light; but when your eye is morally bad, your body is full of darkness. 35. **Take care that the reflected light in you does not come from moral darkness.** 36. If you have light for the body with the absence of darkness, the whole shall be light, as when a candle shines brightly in the dark.* (Luke 11:33-36 EDNT)

Keepers of the Gates

Some years ago, a young Men's Bible Class teacher ran for the U.S. Congress and was elected. It concerned me because we would lose his local influence. He drove from D.C. back to Beckley, WV to teach the class until he was elected to the U.S. Senate. I wrote Robert C. Byrd a letter about his leaving the Bible Class for busy government work, he responded, *"My little light shines brightly in the darkness of Washington, DC."* Later I had the privilege of hearing Senator Byrd speak at a Gideon's meeting. He gave the details about the Great Wall of China.

The wall was 4,160 miles across Northern China and a structure large enough to be seen from the moon with the naked eye. Wall construction started as far back as Chinese recorded history. Prisoners of war, convicts, soldiers, farmers and civilians provided the labor. Many Chinese stories speak of parted lovers and men dying of starvation and disease working on the construction. Materials used for the wall, were whatever could be found nearby: clay, stone, willow branches, reeds, sand and the bodies of the dead.

Bribing the Keepers of the Gates

Everyone listened closely as Senator Byrd told of the years it took to build the wall and the cost of material and lives. Particularly, how workers who died on the job were entombed in the wall. The wall was built to keep China's enemies from attacking sections of the country. History reveals that the wall worked well when the country was strong. Only when a dynasty was weakened from within, were invaders able to advance and conquer. In the many years since the wall was completed, not a single invader ever breached the wall; they did not have to scale or break it down, they simply bribed **the keepers of the gates**.

Parents are the Keepers of the Gates

Families are the last line of defense against Satan's onslaughts against the faith-based entities and the true worship of God. Strong leadership in the home is the last bulwark to protect the beacon of light coming from the lampstands we call "church." In reality, no wall of protection is stronger than the individuals who guard the gates. It is not whether or not the faith-based movement is strong enough to protect the ongoing kingdom ministry; the real question is where are the men to stand in the gap and guard the gates of the family and keep the home fires burning to shine light on both the strength and weakness of the family unit. When strong men are on guard at home, the lampstand in the houses of worship will shine and the Kingdom of God will advance. Strong families make strong and well supported places of worship.

*23. **But be on guard**: behold, I have forewarned you about every-thing. 24. But in those days, after the time of trouble, **the sun shall be darkened, and the moon will give no reflected light**,* (Mark 1:23-24 EDNT)

*21. **When a strong man is armed and guards his homestead, his goods are safe**: 22. But when*

a stronger one overpowers him, he takes all the
weapons in which he trusted, and divides up the
plunder. 23. He who is not with me is against me: and
those who do not gather the sheep, scatters them.
(Luke 11:22-23 EDNT)

Opportunity Equals Obligation

The death of Muhammad Ali was a shock
to America. I did not want to advance this issue
until Muhammad Ali had been honored for his
achievements in life. However, watching his funeral
Ceremony, it appeared that Ali was recognized by
the world as a man of faith. Then I remembered the
words a friend shared years ago about Cassias Clay/
Muhamad Ali. Lewis J. Willis, sat by Muhammad
Ali on a flight out of Atlanta soon after the boxer
converted to Islam and changed his name. Mr. Willis,
an editor seeking a story, asked him why he made the
switch from Christianity to Islam. His response was
shocking: ***"There was no challenge in Christianity;***
Islam gave me a way to change the world."

Who Failed Cassias Clay?

Muhammad Ali was confident in his statement,
firm in his conviction, and satisfied with his decision.
Who failed Cassias Clay? In his hour of glory, he
made a drastic switch from the teachings of his
Christian Mother. Did someone fail to lead him to
a personal experience with Christ? Who missed an
opportunity to harness this strong voice as a fervent
witness for Christianity? Where was the man of the
house? Where was the mother's pastor? Where were
the teachers, coaches, and friends?

Missed Opportunity

True believers can change the world one person and one day at a time. The big question, *"How many other Mother's sons will slip through the cracks and become a spokes-person for another religion?"* Christianity must compete for the minds, souls and hearts of the young in the marketplace to remain viable in the Twenty-first Century. What about missed opportunities? What have you done recently to advance the Cause of Christ? Do you know a young person in your community or your faith-based worship who needs guidance to become a follower of Jesus? Don't miss an opportunity to witness to God's saving grace. The old adage remains true, *"Opportunity equals obligation."*

A New Creation

The Christian faith provides a means to change **individuals and the world.** *"Therefore, if any man be in Christ, he is a new creation: observe, the old things have passed away; all things have become new.* (2 Corinthians 5:17 EDNT) True conversion works. Anything less is not valid Christianity. The only hope for a viable mono-theistic, faith-based worship and witness is an internal redirection of the heart and soul that brings with it a missional lifestyle and personal protest against the immorality of society. Such redirection will bring both a commitment to the cardinal tenets of sacred writings and a spirit of cooperation and teamwork among the people.

A Basic Tenant of Christianity

Recently in Trinidad a young Hindu asked, **"Why does your religion not teach reincarnation?"** My simple answer, *"A basic tenant of Christianity is Reincarnation." "You see, 'if anyone be in Christ, he is a new creation, old things have passed away and all things have become new.' As Believers, we fix our eternal destiny before death.... there is certainty as to our place in eternity."* When Paul was writing the second personal letter to the converts of Corinth, he was clear that looking at the Cross through the Empty Tomb enabled a better understanding of the new creation in and through Jesus Christ. The Resurrection of Christ which guaranteed His Deity became the foundation for the "new creation" at conversion.

> *16. In conclusion, we should know no one after the flesh: I affirm that we have known Christ after the flesh, yet henceforth we know Him no more as a mortal man.* Paul explained the "new creation" and the missional work of believers: *17.* **Therefore if any man be in Christ, he is a new creation: observe, the old things have passed away; all things have become new. 18. All things are of God, who has brought us together in Himself by Jesus Christ, and has given to us the ministry of bringing people together; 19. how that God was in Christ bringing together the world to Himself, not counting their false steps and blunders against them; and has committed us to speak intelligent words that bring man and God together.** (2 Corinthians 5:16-19 EDNT)

No Simple Solutions Only Wise Choices

There are no simple answers, because secular economics and materialistic enterprises have locked up the secrets and thrown away the keys. The wealth managers, entrepreneurs of business have buried the combination code to prosperity deep within the pages of mathematical formula and academic textbooks that require years of specialized knowledge to open the doors.

A Fresh View of the Process

Notwithstanding the complication of economics, faith-based people must not see the complication but take a fresh view of the sophistication of the process. The secrets, the keys, and the combination code to prosperity are all clearly presented in sacred writings. Using God's Plan is free. God's written material is not locked away in a bank vault or catalogued in a public library; it is open for daily perusing. God's Word is freely offered for consistent study and persistent practice: good results of the effort are promised to all who will read, listen believe and learn.

Provided family and friends agree to
walk together on the right path, good
things are bound to happen.

VIII

Agreeing
To Walk Together

Walk Along with Me

Sacred writings are clear that two walking together in God's Light would have fellowship with God and each other and would live a life cleansed from sin and would not walk in the shadows of immorality and economic despair. Faith-based couples desiring communion, partnership, friendship, and communication that includes a sense of stewardship with God and each other must walk together in God's Light and not in the shadows of materialism. If they desire to raise children in the fear and admonition of God, they must agree to walk together cautiously and be fully aware of God's clear guidance. Each parent **must take care that their reflected light does not come from moral darkness.** (Luke 11:35)

> 5. This then is the message which we have heard of Him, and announce to you, that God is light, and no darkness can find a place in Him. 6. If we say that we have fellowship with Him, and at the same time walk in darkness, we lie, and are not living the truth: 7. **but if we walk in the light, as He is in the light, we have fellowship one with another, and the**

blood of Jesus Christ <u>His</u> Son cleanses <u>us</u> from all sin. <u>8. If we say that we have no sin, we deceive ourselves, and the truth is not in us. 9. If we admit our sins, faithful is He and righteous in order that He may cleanse us from all wickedness. 10. If we deny that we have sinned, it means that we are treating Him as a liar; and that His word does not dwell in our hearts.</u> (1 John 1:5-7 EDNT)

The Father's Business

Does this mean that parents are to be perfect? Of course not, parents are subject to human weakness. What it does mean is that two people must *"agreed to come together and learn to walk together in God's light;"* it is a "learning experience" not an absolute fault-free process*. **"Can two people walk together without agreeing on the direction?*** (Amos 3:3 NIV) When parents are living a cleansed life in fellowship with God and each other, their children will have a chance to serve God and have an opportunity for a blessed future. Such a family lifestyle qualifies parents for leadership in the Father's Business that Jesus spoke of at the Temple*. **And He said to them, Why did you search for Me? Know you not that I must be about My Father's business?*** (Luke 2:49) The Father's Business advances the kingdom. The Father's Business is family business. Participation then is sanctified and God's work on earth develops and moves forward.

Financial Shortfall or Family Problems

It is clear to this writer that faith-based entities do not have a financial shortfall or budget deficit;

they normally have families who need to improve their relationship with God and with each other. Such difficulties will hinder full commitment to God and must be fixed before adequate participation and support are available for God's work. The spirituality of the family has a direct relationship to the financial wholeness of both the family and places where families worship. When credit is misused, and debt becomes burdensome, or there is disagreement on how funds are to be allocated, both the family and the place of worship will suffer loss. As the pristine church in Jerusalem grew, a need for lay leadership developed and the congregation was instructed to seek individuals with an honest report, completely influenced by the Holy Spirit and wisdom, to be assigned to the task at hand. As a result of this participation *"the word of God increased; and the number of disciples grew rapidly."* (Acts 6:1-8 EDNT)

Trusted Caretakers

Later when the requirements were codified, the stipulation included faithfulness in marriage, not accused of reckless living, and with children under parental control. They were to be good stewards beyond reproach, not stubborn or self-willed, not easily angered, not given to wine, not greedy for money, and holding to the faithful Word. (Titus 1:5-9; 1 Timothy 3:1-7) The same requirements were for both parents: male and female. The clear understanding was if parents could not take care of their household how could they be trusted to be caretakers for places of worship.

A Personal Word

Early in our marriage, Gail and I were having some difficulty communicating about something important. One day, in the heat *of "a failure at communication,"* she said*, "I'm just not going to talk with you until we learn to communicate!"* We laughed about the matter. How were we going to learn to communicate if we did not talk? We learned, and life got better day by day and year by year. The family motto now is *"**Come and walk along with me, the best is yet to be**!"* We enjoy the present moment and try to fix things as they "come loose." Try it; it works and also improves your relationship with God!

We have three plaques hanging in the entry hall of our home at Morning Air Estate at Lone Mountain. One was purchased when we were first married and reads, *"**Love spoken here!**"* Another is a framed needlepoint by Gail's aunt, Katherine Womble*;* *"**Called to listen to the needs of others; even those unspoken.**"* The final plaque was written by Jewish Rabbi Ben Ezra and reads:

> *Grow old along with me*
> *The best is yet to be.*
> *The last of life for which the first was made*
> *Our times are in His hands.*

Shedding Scriptural Light on Family Division

Sacred writings inform the question that two walking together in God's light would reflect that light on each other and they would share *koninea*. This word is translated **sharing, participation, communion, and stewardship**, in reality the concept of *koninea* points to participating in something in which others also participates or "fellowship." It describes a kind of mutual involvement or participation in spiritual matters. This is what a faith-based family does around the kitchen table and at a place of worship. The influence of parents and grandparents extends far into the future. When parents and grandparents pray for the family, God hears every prayer even when the prayer is no longer prayed. *"The prayer you no longer pray God heard."* (Luke 1:13 EDNT)

> 9. **Two are better than one, because they have a good return for their labor:** 10. *if either of them falls down, one can help the other up. But pity anyone who falls and has no one to help them up. 11. Also, if two lie down together, they will keep warm. But how can one keep warm alone? 12.* **Though one may be over-powered, two can defend themselves. A cord of three strands is not quickly broken.** (Ecclesiastes 4:9-6:12 NIV)

God's Concern for Dysfunctional Parents

Four times in the Old Testament God demonstrates His concern for biological parents who fail to function adequately in their divinely ordained role as spouse and parent: Exodus 20:5; 34:7, Numbers 14:18; and Deuteronomy 5:9. *"Keeping mercy for thousands, forgiving iniquity and transgression and* sin, *and* that will by no means clear the guilty; **visiting the iniquity of the fathers (parents) upon the children, and** upon the childrenᵻs children, unto the ***third and*** to the ***fourth generation***. Obviously, the present problems of the family are extended into the future as difficulties for and with the children.

Consequence of Sinful Lifestyle on Children

Parental alienation is a process where children develop unwarranted fear, disrespect or hostility towards the family and others. The Old Testament had a strong statement about the consequence of parental failures and the impact of a sinful lifestyle on the children: *"the sins of *fathers being visited on the children and the children's children to the third and fourth generation."* (Exodus 34:7; Numbers 14:18) Taken at face value, it seems harsh and heartless; however, the New Testament provides through Jesus forgiveness and redemption for the whole household. Yet, this is not the only positive reflecting of light on this generational curse. The converse of the statement is also true. This means that good parenting can break the curse of past generations and with faith-based teaching provide children an opportunity to choose the right path toward a spiritual lifestyle. Children should be made a moral citizen of the world to prepare them to become mystical citizens of Heaven.

The Converse is Correct

A converse is *"a theorem formed by interchanging the hypothesis and conclusion of a set of data."* The converse of this negative statement is true and has a more positive implication: that is, since the sins of a *parent has evil influence – then the righteous living and guidance of a *parent would influence children toward the right path in life.

Create a Positive Legacy

This then is the positive converse statement: **the righteousness of parents will influence children and grand-children for four generations.** This becomes a positive spiritual legacy! Each converted parent begins a new and exciting positive legacy for their children and future generations. The New Testament has a positive take on this issue. Parents may start a new legacy by walking with the Lord before their children and this spiritual heritage can live for four generations. *And fathers provoke not your children to anger: but nurture them in the discipline and instruction of the Lord.* (Ephesians 6:4 EDNT)

---

*It would do no damage to scripture to translate "father" as "parent" because: *28. In Christ there is neither Jew nor Greek, bond nor free, male or female; for you are all one in Christ Jesus. 29. And if you belong to Christ, then you are Abraham's offspring and Abraham's promise is your promise.* (Galatians 3:28-29 EDNT)

God's Plan and Satan's Strategy

From the foundation of the world, God ordered and ordained three basic institutions to produce, protect, and preserve individuals. First, God initiated a family in a lush garden and almost immediately Satan's strategy was to plunder God's handiwork. Because of the failure of Adam and Eve to learn from their daily walk with God in the cool or each day, their children were thrust into a harsh world and did not clearly understand how to worship God. *"...the life of the flesh is in the blood: and I have given it to you upon the altar to make an atonement for your souls: for it is the blood that makes an atonement for the soul."* and *"without the shedding of blood there was no redemption.* (Leviticus 17:11; Hebrews 9:22) One son brought a vegetable offering from his garden and the other son presented a lamb from his flock. God accepted the blood-sacrifice but rejected the bloodless one. We all know the rest of the story and Satan's plunder strategy remains in full force against modern families and ultimately all faith-based efforts to bring the message of Grace to a world lost in the wilderness of economic materialism.

God ordained and ordered three basic institutions for human development. Each basic institution is related to the **Individual**. A philosophy of life begins with and awareness of these three basic institutions were intended and structured by Divine Providence for the benefit of families and children. They are the (1) **nuclear family**, (2) **formally constituted community**, and (3) **faith-based entities.** These three primary entities are interrelated and cannot survive alone. Providence designed the physical anatomy of human beings so that individuals would be **produced** within an established nuclear family, **protected** in a formally, constituted community, and **preserved** in the context of both family and community through the influence of a faith-based entity.

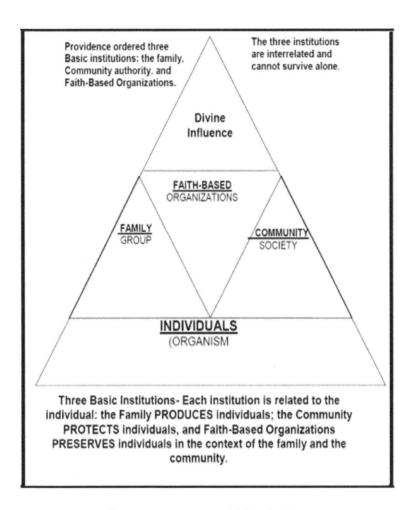

Providence ordered three Basic institutions: the family, Community authority, and Faith-Based Organizations.

The three institutions are interrelated and cannot survive alone.

Divine Influence

FAITH-BASED
ORGANIZATIONS

FAMILY
GROUP

COMMUNITY
SOCIETY

INDIVIDUALS
(ORGANISM

Three Basic Institutions- Each institution is related to the individual: the Family PRODUCES individuals; the Community PROTECTS individuals, and Faith-Based Organizations PRESERVES individuals in the context of the family and the community.

Cornerstone and Linchpins

The family is the cornerstone and parents are the linchpins used by God to keep the wheels of civilized progress moving forward for the children. Otherwise Satan will surely derail the whole system and continue to search and destroy God's handiwork. The family is God's prevention against immorality and the means of **producing individuals** to be matured through nurturing care and education from Godly parents.

The community **protects individuals** and makes available the means/resources for their protection and stability. Finally, the Faith-based entities are to **preserve all individuals** in the context of their family, community and Faith-based worship.

Families are Building Blocks

Since families are the building blocks of both society and religion, good families make good churches; not the other way around. The early church was instructed to choose as leaders good and stable family men. This was before the church got in the business of thinking programs could build families. In fact, church programming tends to separate families and establish a mindset contrary to church growth, by permitting the children and adolescents to be separated into small groups outside the leadership of the pastor and the main worship experience. The building blocks of the family are confession, conversion, communion, collect, common-sense communication, and common family worship.

Good and Bad Legacies

Faith-based groups become a reflection of the families within their membership. When controversy and friction are present in the home, it complicates the faith-based witness. To make Christianity viable in the future, there must be a drastic change in the thinking about families and this includes support and guidance for those seeking marriage and those who may be having relationship difficulties. When the right attitude about personal and kingdom finance is not taught by example, one may predict real struggles in the lives of the young when they leave the nest and start a family of their own. Both good and bad legacies continue for generations unless they are interrupted by good parenting and a Divine encounter that brings about personal conversion with a deep commitment to a spiritual lifestyle that honors the cause of Christ.

Time Complicates the Entanglement

The longer the entanglement with evil continues the more difficult it is to turn young people around. The youthful time in the byways of sin are never ignored by God nor are the marks of sin removed from the body or the mind, but the soul may be refreshed and redeemed. The visiting of both negative and positive influence of parents has a fixed time during a child's youthful years. Perhaps the scripture is referring to the young being led astray by the influence of a sinful parent, but as they grow and mature they may realize the problem and turn to Jesus for revitalization and redemption. There is light at the end of the tunnel, but there may also be light at the beginning of the tunnel when the light of sacred scripture is focused on the right path for the young.

Teach the young how they should live; when they are older they will remember. (Proverbs 22:6 EDOT)

27. No man can break into a strong man's house and plunder his goods, unless he first binds the strong man; and then he can plunder his house. (Mark 2:27 EDNT)

14. For the unbelieving husband is separated from immorality by the wife, and the unbelieving wife is separated from immorality by the husband: else their children would be defiled (corrupted, contaminate); but now the children are consecrated. (1 Corinthians 7:14 EDNT)

Parental Influence

Parental influence on a child begins long before birth. In fact, from ancient times the Chinese culture has considered a child to be nine (9) months old at birth. All life develops through stages and this process is initiated at conception based on the DNA of parental ancestors. This is where the heritage of both parents combines and creates the beginning of life. The previous three or four biological generations of both parents influence the DNA structure of a child. Specialized periods of development begin with incubation in the womb and continue through infancy, childhood and adolescence.

Intercessory Prayer

Sharing a Prayer program in St. Croix, USVI, my topic was the value of intercessory prayer emphasizing that one could not pray for others without receiving a blessing themselves. Children understand the pulpit message even if parents do not! At the close of a Sunday through Wednesday meeting, a young girl, about 10 and new to Christianity, wrote me a letter: "Dear Dr. Green, I like your preaching. I like stories about people's lives. I enjoyed Mrs. Green's singing; it was warm and soft and comfortable. *And prayer is just like jam. You can't spread even a little without getting some on yourself.*" She clearly understood the value and benefits of intercessory prayer. Believing families and their children create a strong force for good.

Good Parenting makes a Difference

In the process of growing a family, good parenting can make a significant difference in the outcome. Although a child is born with a sinful nature that will lead them in a negative direction, good parenting can guide their feet to the right path. Even the slightest weakness of parenting will have a negative impact on a child's upbringing. Many things are learned by a child prior to birth. The sounds they hear, the mother's emotions, even the mother's diet and habits influence the development of a child. In fact, the logical development of a child begins in the lives of both parents prior to conception. At conception, the gene pools of both parents are joined into one entity and the child will have DNA and traits traceable to parents and grandparents. When a child is born, a special human being enters the world, one that is different from all others that have ever or will ever walk this planet. Just as fingerprints; each child is different! Children are constructed from a gene pool that influences their basic traits and are placed in an environment that imprints their behavior. Children will develop in a negative direction without strong and positive parental influence. Their direction depends on the nurturing of parents and the weight of each inherited factor. Parents must understand and be vigilant during each stage of a child's development.

Parental Bonding -Womb to age 3

Human bonding is a special intimacy that develops between parents and a child. This bonding is crucial to the child's development. For most children, this womb to age three bonding relationship is their first and will affect all their future relationship issues. If the bond between parents is one of love and security, then the child is more likely to seek out these healthy elements in future relationships. Children who miss quality infant bonding may grow up without the capacity for love and intimacy; therefore, bonding is the first and primary responsibility of parents when a new child is placed in their home by God. Yes, children are a gift from God; a Divine heritage and a legacy for parents. *"Except God build the house, they who build it labor in vain." "Children are a heritage from the Lord"* (Psalm 127:1-5)

Basic Elements of Personality -Womb to age 5

Personality has elements of character, behavior qualities, and expressions of individuality and is recognizable soon after birth. It is the totality of one's attitudes, interests, physical behavioral patterns, emotional responses, social roles, and other individual traits that endure over time. Much of the building blocks of personality are in place by age 5, but some later events impact the positive development of the adult personality. Some parents unknowingly lead children astray through careless and inconsistent behavior. Such behavior can influence the future action of children for several generations. It seems that patterns of immoral attitudes, disrespectful behavior, and bad habits are passed to children and grandchildren from parents and grandparents (Exodus 20:5).

A Proper Foundation

Childhood is a crucial time for laying the proper foundation. Efforts to explain child development include listing the common characteristics of behavior by age groupings. It should be remembered however that every child will not fit into described patterns. Children grow and develop at different speeds and have a different set of influential factors coming from close family members. This material describes only general behavior and cohort groups often overlap and readily influences values, beliefs, and expectations.

Hereditary Factors

Research over several decades has pointed to hereditary factors, especially the basic emotional tone in the personality. Yet, it is equally evident that the acquisition of values, beliefs, hope, and outlook are greatly influenced by childhood socialization and personal experiences. The gradual acceptance of the standard and practices of another culture influences personality development, because of the process called enculturation, most individuals accept and adopt the traditions, rules, manners, and biases of their surroundings in which they develop and grow. This fact gives parents a major role in personal development of children. Considerable moral and spiritual guidance are required for parenting to produce effectively without loss or waste.

Building a Knowledge Base -Womb to age 7

The knowledge base is made of up the short-term memory of facts, data, and information used to create the long-term memory that produce a relatively permanent competency-based knowledge. Creative or divergent thinking is not done in a vacuum. It depends on and uses a knowledge base. Close observation of the creative thinking processes of children illustrates clearly the critical role of the knowledge base.

Children overtime develop a core competency baseline that feeds a knowledge base upon which they will construct most of the information for a formal education and reading. At age 7 or about the time a child enters the third year of school, the foundation baseline should be established; that is, they should be able to read and write at a grade level in order to proceed higher in the educational structure. The more and better a child reads, the firmer the knowledge base becomes.

Steps In Character Development
Womb to age 9 – fundamental steps in character

Character is the set of affective, cognitive, and behavioral patterns gleaned from life experience that determines how one thinks, feels, and behaves. Character continues to develop throughout life, although much depends on inborn traits and early childhood experiences. Character is also related to the level of moral development. While the debate continues as to which of these provide the most influence, most scholars agree that proper parenting is critical to the development of personality. Parents who can adapt their parenting skills to the temperament and social environment of the child can provide better guidance for good character and development a mature attitude toward the real world.

Keys to Spiritual Formation -Womb to age 11

Just as all the other steps in development, spiritual formation begins before birth and continues through about age eleven. Spiritual formation is influenced by significant events in the life of the child, personal life experiences, parental and adult behavior, observation of peers, and social changes in or near their environment. Parents have become specialists in nutrition. Learning disorders and new guidance techniques have been established. Children are enrolled, coached, and transported to and from school, music lessons, games, practices, social events, and medical appointments, but in many respects, parents are missing the core of the child's needs: personal spirituality. This is where patience, prayer, Bible study, and family worship contribute the most to the future of the young.

The Influence of Peers over Family -(Age 12 – 14)

Parents should never talk directly about spirituality, instead they should watch for an opportunity to cultivate natural interest in honesty, fairness, morality, ethics, and justice. Parents should articulate their own spiritual autobiography or journey and share it with all the family. The vocabulary used and any diversity between behavior and experiences would become obvious. Identify common difficulties such as death of a love one, loss of job, or other experiences that impact the way one thinks about God and justice.

Among the most destructive things that can happen to a child is to become socially involved with peers who have bad habits, immoral behavior and weak character. In the general population, it is difficult to restrict these associations because the restriction has the reverse effect. Early adolescence peer groups have a considerable influence on other children's behavior. Some peer groups are involved in deviant and aggressive behavior while other peer groups have acceptable social behavior.

Associates must be Monitored

This means that the associates of children and adolescents must be monitored, and each negative incident promptly dealt with by a loving parent. This is where the family home environment has an advantage. Parents may control contacts in the home, but when children go to public school the same problems exist as parents have with their children's association with bad company. It becomes necessary to use tough love and explain to a child or adolescent that some associations are bad and unacceptable. Things they want to do and some people with whom they want to associate are in their best interest. Constructive communication is crucial at this point. This presents a real challenge for parents; even more so if they have previously neglected the child's development.

The Influence of Other Adults - (Age 15 – 18)

Notwithstanding, years of care and concern in parenting from womb to 14, this period in the life of the young is most challenging for parents. A sensual society has opened the floodgates to immoral behavior and parents have little opportunity to intervene. Almost any intervention would be considered interfering. Young people hate interference from parents and/or grandparents. Provided early training went well and each stage of life was properly addressed, parents have a chance with love and prayer to make a difference. Other adult role models such as teachers, church leaders, the parents of peers, *et al.* begin to have significant influence on the young. Whatever parents plan to do to prepare children for the real world must be done prior to age 15 or a new and special program and enlist the whole family and the mature of the congregation must be established to deal with and abnormal adolescent behavior. This is not a time to be timid. It is time to attack the strongholds of Satan and take back the moral high ground for the Kingdom.

17. But, beloved, you must remember the words once spoken before of the apostles of our Lord Jesus Christ; 18. How they told you there should **be ridiculing spirits in the last time,** who would make their ungodly appetites into a rule of life. 19. Such are the men who now keep themselves apart; fleshly creatures without the Spirit. 20. *It is for you, beloved, to make your most holy faith the foundation of*

your lives, and to go on praying in the power of the Holy Spirit; 21. maintain yourselves in the love of God, and wait for the mercy of our Lord Jesus Christ, with eternal life as your goal. 22. And some, you must give a hearing and show them to be false; 23. and **others you must pull out of the fire and rescue them;** while you shun them; even the outward fringe of what the flesh has defiled must be hateful to you. 24. Now unto Him who is able to keep you from slipping, and to present you blameless before the presence of His glory with exceeding joy, 25. to the only wise God our Savior, be glory and majesty, dominion and power, before time was, and now, and for all ages. Amen. (Jude 1:17-25 EDNT)

Stop the World I Want to get off! - (Age 19 +)

By age 19 young people have learned the cost of going to school, driving a car, or living in their own place. They often return to parents or grandparents for assistance with school or living expenses. This should not be discouraged. It gives the family a **"second chance"** to influence their future. Once young people have come to the stage of wanting to stop the world and get off, they are usually open to mature and family guidance about the future. The world can be a scary place for young people and unless they have a family anchor they will turn to artificial support that leads to becoming involved with the wrong people.

God-given Opportunity

Parents should see this **"second chance"** as a God-given **opportunity** and an **obligation**. It is probably the last chance the family will have to influence and guide the young person before they take a permanent place in society. Every family should assume that each person will become a constructive and productive member of society. Any negativity passed to a young person at this stage will be counter-productive. Be positive. Philosophy taught that **"one could never reach a positive conclusion beginning with a negative premise."** The old proverb **"accentuate the positive and eliminate the negative"** is still a good guideline for parents, especially at this stage in the lives of young people.

Born with a Sin Nature

All humans are born with a sin nature (Psalm 51:5) because original sin is passed to a child by the parents; the only exception being Jesus who enjoyed a special-case birth. Children are born with more than a potential to sin; it is the inclination of the human nature. (Romans 5:12-21) Yet, through the affection and care of a loving family a child has the opportunity to learn to walk in the ways of the Lord. It is unfortunate that many children do not have a nurturing family and a Faith-based environment to assist them in overcoming the hostile forces from past generations and lessen the inclination toward immorality and away from a spiritual direction. This is where dedicated, God-fearing parenting is required.

24. Some men's sins are plain for all to see and are judged immediately; and some men their sins follow close behind. 25. Even so there are good deeds that are plain to see; and there are deeds that cannot be hidden for long. (1 Timothy 5:24-25 EDNT)

1. Jesus said to His disciples, Crimes against moral standards will come: but serious misfortune to him through whom these crimes come! 2. It would be better for him if dead weights were placed around his neck and he was thrown into the sea, than to hurt a single little one. (Luke 17:1 EDNT)

Edith it's getting Dark!

Part of this technique was learned from my Uncle William. On one occasion William and Edith had a slight disagreement about something. He went outside and sat in a straight chair backward under a tree. As the sun began to go down behind Lone Mountain, he called to the house and said, **"Edith, it's getting dark!"** She ignored him. He called again, but no response from his wife. Evidently, they had agreed to make things right between themselves, according to scripture, **"before the sun goes down."**

> 25. Wherefore speak every man truth with his neighbor without falsehood: for we are members bound one to another. 26. **Have righteous anger without sin: let not the sun go down on your anger: 27. Neither give an opportunity to the devil.** (Ephesians 4:25-27 EDNT)

Being a small child, I did not understand exactly what was happening, and asked their son, Paul, *"What's this all about?"* His response, *"Mom and dad had a little disagreement, and she is teaching him a lesson."* The part about *"Don't let the sun go down on your wrath"* stuck with me through the years. It has certainly increased the sweet fellowship and lessened the *"lack of communication"* between me and Gail.

Knocking Holes in the Darkness

Transparency is a key to happiness in family life. Someone has to dislike the dimness of the night enough to knock some holes in the darkness. Otherwise, our eyes will become accustomed to the night and we tolerate the evil we cannot see. There is a story about an old man in a small town, who they called the "Lamplighter." Early each night he would light the gas lamps at the street corners. The old gas lamps made only a small light on the dark street, but as the he made his rounds it appeared that he was knocking holes in the darkness.

The lamplighter is an example of what one person could do with a little effort. And a good example for family members who daily strive to knock holes in the darkness and enlighten the pathway of family members to see a better way forward for their lives. This is where we stand as Faith-based families. Will you join men and women of good will and take the necessary steps to create a cooperative effort to take back the moral high ground and move the families in your congregation forward into the light of reality. Dare we do less than let God's light shine through us?

Prayer no longer Prayed God Heard

God answers prayers, even those delayed many years. God saw the future and did not judge Zechariah for not fathering a child. Jewish tradition teaches that it was misfortune for a Priest to be childless. Many years Zechariah and Elizabeth had prayed for a child. It was now too late biologically for Elizabeth to conceive a child; therefore, they stopped praying for a son. A Priest without a wife or whose wife was barren was a serious problem in Judaism. Hope for a son may have died, but prayer revitalizes hope and makes real the dreams of things longed for in life. It is never too late for God. One must continue to serve and worship even when answers to important prayers are delayed. The answer will come in due course. ***"The prayer you no longer pray was heard, and Elizabeth shall bear a Son - called JOHN."*** God is prescriptive and precise in answers to prayer. *"The prayer you no longer pray was heard."* Delay is not denial. Parents must hold on to the promises of household salvation…and trust their spiritual legacy will reach the next three or four generations.

God's Plan includes Human Action

Human action is essential for some prayers to be answered. Between God hearing a prayer and the execution of the answer, human action may be required. God's answer to some prayer is worked out in the privacy of your own home. It was a personal consultation between husband and wife that produced the "conception" God promised. Elizabeth hid herself for 5 months until she had visible evidence that God had answered her prayer and removed her reproach. She was waiting for God to make the public announcement – the opposite from the flagrant "name it and claim it" preaching we hear today.

The Effectual and Fervent Prayer

Since nothing is impossible with God, the impossibility must be the lack of faith in the human element or the prayer was for something outside the Will of God. God always answers, sometime God says "Yes" or "No" at other time He simply says "Wait till the time is right" but God always hears and answers the sincere prayer offered in faith. Where two or three are joined together in agreement, the prayer seems to have great potency and urgency. *... husbands, dwell with them according to knowledge, giving honor unto the wife, as unto the weaker vessel, and as being heirs together of the grace of life;* **that your prayers be not hinder**ed. (1 Peter 3:7)

Who is a Saint?

To become a "saint," one must live a holy life separated from the sins of the world, but what is a saint? A young boy was asked this question, and his answer was, "**A Saint is someone the light shines through.**" What he knew about saints was from stained-glass church windows. Each Sunday morning the sun would shine through the paintings of Saints in the stained-glass. Not a bad definition and a rather good understanding. Does God's light shine through you? Do children see the "goodness of a saint" in you? When God's light shines through you to a child, that child sees a real Saint of God! **Take care that the reflected light in you does not come from moral darkness.** (Luke 11:35 EDNT)

Arriving in Lima, Peru on the day the Pope declared several saints were to be taken off the official Vatican list. I searched the streets of Lima for someone who could speak English better than my Spanish. Finally, I found a young man about 25 and asked him about the Pope's decision to take certain Saints off the list. He said it didn't matter, that the people could still pray to them, but the church just wouldn't teach the next generation to recognize them. I asked, *"Why would you want to continue to pray to a saint whom the Pope declared not worthy?"* The young man responded in effect that the idea of Saints was to encourage people to pray, the power was not in the Saint, but in the person praying.

What is a Saint?

A good and reasonable answer so I pushed the conversation, *"What is a Saint, and why does the Church select them?"* He explained that a Saint was someone who lived so well that they bypassed Purgatory and went straight to Heaven when they died. According to his definition and my theology, since I did not accept the concept of purgatory, I was a Saint. I stuck out my hand and said, *"I am Saint Hollis!"* He appeared frightened but did not say a word. He just turned and walked away rapidly. After a few steps, he turned and took another look at me, a few more steps and turned again. He must have believed I was one of the saints that had been defrocked and had appeared to vindicate his position. Observing him as he walked toward the Church down the block, I assumed he would pray or tell his Priest about Saint Hollis.

Shrine to Saint Hollis

Should my travels take me again to Lima, perhaps on that corner I would see a shrine built to Saint Hollis. Whether they build a shrine to me or not, sometimes I feel kind of "saintly." My sons say I feel saintly because I am getting old, losing my hair, and my beard has turned white. If I am not seen as a saint, perhaps I have become a sage. A sage is someone who is regarded as wise and knowledgeable, especially a man of advanced years revered for his wisdom and good judgment. Perhaps I am both, a saint for my religious activities and a sage for my academic adventures. Either way, I am satisfied with myself. Nevertheless, I am both a moral citizen of the world and a mystical citizen of heaven and that is enough! How great is God's goodness to us? As part of the Passover Jewish believers have for each of God's acts of mercy and kindness declared: "*Dayenu* -- **It would have been enough!**"

If God had just brought us out of Egypt and done nothing more;

It would have been enough!

If God had just given us the Torah and done nothing more:

It would have been enough!

If God had just sent the Messiah to us and done nothing more:

It would have been enough!

Walking in Truth

What does stable families, honest businessmen, and Faith-based congregations have to do with kingdom economics and personal wealth? John wrote about the soul in a moral and spiritual sense because Gaius was "walking in truth" in the emphatic and contrasting Gaius' faithfulness with Diotrephes who ridiculed the messenger and rejected the message of truth with a malicious tongue and rejected the brethren. Conflict or disagreements do not produce support for a missional family lifestyle, an honestly operated business, or a spiritual place of worship.

> 2. Beloved, concerning all things I pray that you may **prosper in your occupation or business and be safe and sound in body, as your soul prospers.** 3. For I rejoiced greatly when some brothers came bearing witness of you in truth, as you in truth walk. 4. I have no greater joy than to hear that _my children are walking in truth._ 5. Beloved you are _faithfully serving_ when you show kindness to the brethren, even when they are strangers to you. 6. And they _testify of your love before the assembly:_ if you send them on their journey as godly men, you do well: 7. because they went out for His name's sake, taking nothing from the Gentiles. 8. It is a duty to support such men, that we may show ourselves fellow workers with the truth. (3 John 1:2-8 EDNT)

Blessings Reserved for the Faithful

The blessings of God are reserved for the faithful who walk in truth, work at an occupation or generate funds in a business transaction to enable them to both support their family and humanitarian kingdom needs. Luke's report (Acts 6:3) on the selection of the first leaders to be over *"this **business**;"* It is significant that Paul used the same Greek word (Romans 11:13) ***business/necessity*** when challenging Roman believers about *"distributing to the **necessity** of saints."* Assisting others is a part of God's Business and believers must understand it to be a necessary part of God's work. When the business is done God's way it opens the gateway to both material and spiritual blessings for God's People.

Bring the full tithes into the storehouse,
that there may be food in my house; and
thereby put me to the test, says the Lord
of Hosts, if I will not open the windows of
heaven for you and pour down for you an
over-flowing blessing. I will rebuke the
devourer for you, so that it will not destroy
the fruits of your soil, and your vine in the
field shall not fail to bear,

(Malachi 3:10-11 RSV)

IX

Opening
The Gateway To Blessings

Punctually bring the full tithe into the storehouse, that there may be provisions for My house. Test me on this, says the LORD, and see if I will not throw open the floodgates of heaven and pour out a great blessing that there will not be room enough to store it. (Malachi 3:10 EDOT)

Opening the Gateway to Benefits

A *benefit* is special advantage or privilege possessed by a group or individual. *Privilege* with benefits is an advantage granted or available only to those who participate willingly in an endeavor. An *advantage* is something regarded as a rare or particular benefit. Knowledge resting upon a justified sacred scriptural foundation is the gateway to believer's benefits.

Primitive People are not Poor

In my global travels and the study of societies and social groups, the privilege to meet primitive people who seemed to have a good handle on life and the process of living. Without electricity, running water, air conditioning, vehicles, refrigerators, fine clothing, or an elegant home and ready cash, they were happy, wearing clean clothes and considered themselves to be "wealthy." Why, because they had "enough" to survive and live a normal and relatively peaceful life. To describe them as "poor" would be insulting and would miss the point of their self-sufficiency.

Wealth in the New Testament means "enough", "wages", "living" and self-sufficiency and the word "rich" is not adequate to describe a life blessed by God. God's blessings create opportunities to secure/earn daily bread for the family, put a roof over their heads, and acquire the necessary things to keep the household, farm, or business working. Whatever we receive in the way of external circumstances really comes from a divine source or intervention and does not have "Made in the USA or China." Look closely and you will find, *"Made in the Kingdom of Heaven."* God is good and all He does for mankind is good. The same as at Creation when God looked at His handiwork, He said, *"It is good!"* God's blessings do not come with sorrow or regret, although mental and physical labor is normally required; however, a God-sent blessing does not have the same liabilities as ill-gotten gains of the rich. *"No good comes from ill-gotten wealth, but righteousness rescues from death."* (Proverb 10:2 EDOT)

Personal Involvement

Work is required to earn daily bread, but slave-type labor or dangerous work that disables the mind or body is unnecessary. Earning funds by sweat means physical effort not dangerous or physically debilitating labor. When such risks are required, God is not in it. Those who make merchandise of the poor through physical labor; such as, working with dangerous chemicals, asbestos, black lung risks, or backbreaking effort, are willing to hurt others while enriching themselves. This is not "crumbs" from the Master's Table; it is garbage from the dung hill! Believers deserve and are promised the "Children's Bread" and a seat at God's Table, but not without physical involvement in energy exchange. Those who have others earning funds to support the household must find a way through volunteerism to become actively involved in God's work. There are no "freebees" or entitlement for able-bodied individuals. Yes, believers are freed from sin and hell, but there is no exemption or enfranchisement that eliminates the necessity for physical or mental work. God does not bless idleness or laziness. ***No one can serve two masters God and money***. (Luke 16:13 EDNT)

Privilege with Blessings

Abram was born, some 2,000 years after Adam, and it is most difficult to calculate the years until Abram tithed to Melchizedek. All we know is that tithing was not mentioned until the end of Leviticus although various offerings were commanded to teach God's lessons of financial responsibility and wealth. The "*concept of tithing*" can best be appraised by considering its development within the biblical record. Sacred scriptural record showed that tithing was a privilege with blessings for Abram when he tithed to Melchizedek. Once the true biblical model is clearly understood, all things relative to kingdom economy and personal wealth will work for the benefit of Faith-based families, the blessing of spiritual worship, and the advancement of kingdom outreach.

First Citation is Noteworthy

Normally, the first citation in scripture is a noteworthy explanation: recorded in Genesis 14:18-20, Abram freely gave a tenth of all his gains to Melchizedek. It is significant that Melchizedek was the Priest of the Most High God and the priest brought forth *"bread and wine"* and blessed Abram. After this blessing, Abram voluntarily shared a tenth of all.

> *18. When Melchizedek king of Salem brought out* **bread and wine**, *he was priest of God Most High, 19. and* **he blessed Abram**, *saying, Blessed be Abram by God Most High, Creator of heaven and earth. 20. And praise be to God Most High, who delivered your enemies into your hand.* **Then Abram gave him a tenth of everything.** (Genesis 14:18-20 NIV)

Validation

This scriptural citation validates the tithe was voluntarily given after *"bread and wine* and *blessings"* from the Priest Melchizedek. This deliberate gift produced great benefits for Abram, his family, and his colleagues. Abram kept nothing of the spoils personally, not even a thread or a shoelace, but gave all to the King of Sodom, except the portion he shared with those who traveled with him. His gifts firmly established that Abram was wealthy, because he had *"more than enough"* to share with others. The sharing of material goods with others beyond the needs of family obligations supports wealth as **more than enough--overage** that becomes a wellspring to open the floodgates of blessings.

The Psalmist Remembered

David, the Psalmist, wrote, <u>*In my long memory,*</u> *I* **have never seen the righteous abandoned** *or their* **young denied the children's bread.** (Psalm 37:25 EDOT) Conceivably, David recalled in Psalms that God told Moses Israel would *become "a kingdom of priests and a holy nation"* (Exodus 19:6) when he and his men were hungry and entered the House of God and ate the consecrated bread only allowed for the priests. (1 Samuel 21:6-8) Perhaps the fact that Jesus defended David's action (Mark 2:23-26; Luke 6:1-4) was a foreshadowing of the New Testament tenet about the "Priesthood of Believers" where all who follow Christ become priests before God and are allowed a seat at the table with access to the children's bread. (1 Peter 2:5) Experience is a great teacher. When we see God's blessings on others, we should remember we are included. An old Chinese proverb speaks to this issue: **I hear, and I forget, I see, and I remember, I do, and I understand.** The more involved we are in God's work, the more we understand and remember.

Right Standing and Walking

Once the congregation is in right standing and walking in fellowship with God, showers of blessings will be launched for others and assure support for taking Christ's cleansing word to the church: *"that*

He might consecrate and purify the church with the cleansing water of the word. (Ephesians 5:26 EDNT) So, together, the congregation could participate in taking the message of saving Grace to a lost and thirsty world. *Christ is devoted to the church and gave Himself for it; 26. that He might consecrate and purify it with the cleansing water of the word, 27.* **that He might present the church to Himself as a glorious bride, without spot, wrinkle or blemish.** (Ephesians 5:26-27 EDNT)

No Acceptable Excuses

Obligation with penalty for the lack of punctuality was the Old Testament construct of tithing. There were no acceptable excuses for failure to participate in God's Plan. There were no opportunities to select the best or redeem a selected animal designated for sacrifice. No one could claim the distance was too far to transport their tithe of animals and/or produce. They were instructed to exchange the tithe for silver and carry the silver to the designated place. Obligation with penalty was the condition of being morally or legally bound to do something. Obligation is a course of action to which a person is morally or legally bound: a duty or commitment. Penalty is a punishment or payback imposed for breaking a law, rule, or contract. It may also be considered a disadvantage or handicap imposed on someone typically for infringement of the rules. Yet, the Old Testament regulations were clear, easy to follow, and brought with them a definite benefit.

*30. A tithe of everything from the land, whether grain from the soil or fruit from the trees, belongs to the LORD; it is holy to the LORD. 31. Whoever would redeem any of their tithe must **add a fifth of the value to it.** 32. Every tithe of the herd and flock-every tenth animal that passes under the rod of the Shepherd will be holy to the LORD. 33. **No one may pick out the good from the bad or make any substitution.** If anyone does make a substitution, both the animal and its substitute become holy and cannot be redeemed. 34. These are the commands the LORD gave Moses at Mount Sinai for the Israelites.* (Leviticus 27:30-34 NIV)

24 *But if that place is too distant and you have been blessed by the LORD your God and **cannot carry your tithe** (because the place where the LORD will choose to put his Name is so far way **25** then **exchange your tithe for silver and take the silver with you and go to the place the LORD your God will choose.*** (Deuteronomy 14:24-25)

Obligation with Penalty

Any delay or buy back of the tithe required adding 20% of the value to the tithe. With all the tithing regulations, plus the special gifts required for the Tabernacle and the Levites, giving was estimated to be at least 22% of all possessions. The Old Testament model was clearly: obligation with penalty for non-performance or delay.

16. And he shall make restitution for the harm that he has done in regard to the holy thing and shall add one-fifth to it and give it to the priest. So, the priest shall make atonement for him with the ram of

the trespass offering, and it shall be forgiven him.
Leviticus 5:16)

Material Wealth

The concept of personal "material wealth" comes primarily from the writings of the Old Testament economy and primarily dealt with property, land, animals, and produce. (Proverbs 13:22) However, both Old and New Testament deals with good people leaving an inheritance for their family and grandchildren and warned that ill-gotten wealth would be left to the hands of others. Paul in writing to Timothy explained that should anyone not work and provide for their own people, especially their family, they were denying the faith and were worse than an infidel. (I Timothy 5:8) Perhaps the old adage, *"An idle mind is the devil's workshop,"* was based on (Proverbs 16:27-30). Perhaps present-day believers should be reminded that God's injunction *"man would earn his bread by the sweat of his face"* (Genesis 3:19) has not been rescinded. Also, Paul's command to the church at Thessalonica has not been annulled: **"No work—no eat!"**

> *10. When we were with you we instructed you that **if any would not work, neither should they eat.** 11. For we understand that some among you **behave in an undisciplined manner refusing to work at all, but interfere in others affairs.** 12. Now with the authority of the Lord Jesus Christ, **we urge such people to attend quietly to their own affairs and earn their own bread.** (2 Thessalonians 3:10-12 EDNT)*

*8. **If anyone provides not for his own people, and especially his family,** <u>he has denied the faith, and is worse than an unbeliever</u>.* (1 Timothy 5:8 EDNT)

Opportunity with Blessing

Opportunity with Blessing was the New Testament believers chance to have a seat at the table and participate in the ongoing ministry of making disciples, planting churches, and supporting those who were on the front line of advancing the kingdom. Gentiles were given a seat at the Table with access to the children's bead. The failure to be seated created *"the loss of potential gain."* Opportunity cost in economics means *"the next-highest-valued alternative use of that resource"* Since all resource (land, money, time, etc.) has alternative uses, every action, choice, or decision has an associated opportunity cost.   A benefit/resistance value of something is that which must be given up to acquire or achieve something else.

Back to Privilege with Benefits

When kingdom economy and personal wealth becomes the concern of present-day believers, local congregations are in a hard place. It is evident that the whole Biblical record and the meaning of conversion, disciple making, church planting, and the believer's missional lifestyle is not clearly understood. The New Testament does not require tithing, but freewill giving under the new Covenant. God mentioned no specific amount to believers; however, tithing seems to be a good starting point or measuring stick for giving. The discipline of grace and understanding the needs of family, the kingdom, and the poor determine the value of proportional giving of tithes and offerings.

Under New Testament grace, divinely provided wealth is stored safely in the Kingdom Bank, where thieves cannot break in and steal, not in individual pockets or wallets.

> *He who is faithful in small things is trustworthy in big things. 11. If you have not been faithful in managing personal resources, who will trust you with true riches?* (Luke 16:10, 11 EDNT) *But we have this treasure in earthen vessels that the all-prevailing greatness of the power may be of God, and not from us.* (2 Corinthians 4:7 (EDNT) *For where your treasure is, there your heart will be also.* (Luke 12:34 EDNT. Here we miss the Greek emphasis *"Where your **heart** is, there your_**treasure** will also be."* Personal wealth is not about the amount of the coinage value of money; it is about the value of individuals committed to God's Will and their attitude about the needs of Kingdom activities.

> *14. When they arrived, they said, Teacher, we know that you are true, and fear no man: for you regard not the person of men, but truly teach the way of God:* **Is it lawful to pay tribute to Caesar? 15. Shall we hand over tribute or not? But He, knowing their hypocrisy, replied, Why try to ensnare Me? Fetch Me a coin that I may see it.** *16 And they brought one. And He asked, Whose image and superscription is this? And they answered, Caesar's. 17.* **And Jesus said, Present to Caesar the things that are Caesar's, and present to God the things that are God's. And they stood amazed.**
> *(Mark 12:13-17 EDNT)*

"Enough"

From personal experience, it seems that regardless of individual income, the amount left is usually zero. The material system normally takes all the income of the poor. W. L. Prichard once shared with Mercer University students a simple plan for managing personal resources. *"Give the first-tenth to the Lord; use the next eight-tenths for the obligations of life, and save the last-tenth and you will always have something for special gifts. Whoever follows this formula will have high satisfaction and the respect of both God and man."* The concept and the word "wealth" is rarely used in the New Testament and normally means either *"enough," "income," "purchase power," or funds required for living"*. See Acts 18:3 *"And because he was of the same trade, he lodged and worked with them: for by their occupation they were tent makers."* And in Acts 19:25 Paul explained *"...by this craft we have our **livelihood**."*

Gifts Measured by Cost to the Giver

Sacred Writings demonstrate that Jesus valued gifts in terms of the giver. Measuring totals and assessing the remainder seems to be the keys to understand the Divine use of personally controlled funds. Tithing, for example, is calculated by the amount of earned income; while gifts are valued by the amount remaining under individual control. The highest authority on the subject is Jesus as recorded in the Gospel of Mark:

> *41. And **Jesus sat down in front of the collection-box, and observed** the people dropping money into*

*the chests: and **many that were rich cast in much. 42. But one widow dropped in two copper coins out of her poverty,** worth about a penny. 43. And Jesus called His disciples, saying I assure you, **this poor widow has given more than all they who gave to the treasury: 44.** <u>For they all put in of their abundance; but she gave all she had, even all her living.</u>* (Mark 12:41-44 EDNT)

God knows your Deadlines

My mother, as a widow with three children, often said something similar to: *"God knows your deadlines."* because of the death of a young husband, mother often faced financial crisis on a daily and/or weekly basis. On one occasion, I remember a Thursday supper when mother said, *"This is the last of the food until I get paid on Friday."* Having to give up her career, because teachers were paid only eight and one-half months a year, which left the summer with no money for food or rent. On the occasion mentioned above, I ran home from school the next afternoon to see how God had answered mother's prayer. After searching the porch, house and icebox and finding nothing, I sat down on my bed in despair. Then I spotted a crisp FIVE DOLLAR bill sticking out from under a small bedside lamp. In 1945, **$5.00** had the 2018 buying power of **$69.25**. God had extraordinarily met mother's deadline.

As a young minister living in Atlanta, I awoke one morning thinking, ***"I need $512 to meet payments due today."*** Remembering mother's statement about "deadlines," I rested easy. The phone rang.

An unknown voice asked *"Are you the Hollis Green who wrote Why Churches Die?"* Answering in the affirmative, the caller proceeded *"I will be in Atlanta about 11:30 today, could we have lunch?"* I met the gentleman and had a pleasant lunch and conversation about his recent Faith-based conversion. His difficulty was his vocabulary; being ex-Navy and in the construction business, he was prone to angry cursing. As a young Christian, he wanted to clean up his language before meeting God. I suggested using a few words from the Game of Monopoly when he was upset. Instead of curse words, he was instructed to say, *"Go to jail, don't pass go and don't collect $200."* He thought others would laugh at him for that tactic but was willing to try. He was told that usually it would take about 21 days to begin to create a new vocabulary for use when one was angry. He was willing to try.

About three weeks later he called again, *"Mr. Green, you will be pleased. This morning an employee's action cost my company $2,000.* I simply said with a smile, "Don't pass go and don't collect $200. *He was a good worker and without the changes in my lifestyle, he would have been cursed out and fired. God is good!"*

The God Thing!

Oh, I may have missed sharing the *"God thing"* that happened during lunch. He reached across the table and placed a folded check in my shirt pocket. My thoughts were directed to *"God knows my deadlines."* Naturally curious on the way home I checked the check: it was $500. **[In 2018 value that was worth $2,428.06.]** Yet, my human weakness showed, I said aloud, *"But God I needed $512."* Stopping by my Atlanta PO Box there was a check from a Florida court where I had been called for a jury pool (after I moved). Even though I was never called for duty, the Court was obligated to pay $10. It had been several years and with interest the enclosed check was $11.39. Again, I thought,...."*God I needed $512."* Checking the parking change in my car, I found the balance. God had met my deadline! How easy it is to forget the wisdom of parents and the affection God has for His children. Believers do not have to eat the "scraps" from the table, because we have a seat at the table and have access to the children's bread. Now I had **"enough and then some"** for my daily needs. According to kingdom economics and the New Testament understanding of personal wealth—I was wealthy!

Mother's Reserve

Mother was concerned that she would pass with unpaid bills and she instructed my sister to wait 90 days after her homegoing to see if any bill came before she divided the balance left in the bank. She paid attention to the scripture: *8. **Owe no man anything, but to love one another: for he that loveth another hath fulfilled the law.*** (Romans 13:8 KJV) When Mother passed, and all her bills were paid, the balance in her account was $3,009 to be divided between her three children. I placed my one-thousand and three dollars in a special envelope marked MOTHER'S RESERVE.

> *5. Therefore you must line up under authority, not only to escape God's anger, but also because it is the right thing to do. 6. For this cause also* **pay your taxes***: for the authorities are God's ministers, devoting themselves to this work. 7.* **Pay what you owe: taxes to whom taxes are due; custom duties to whom payment is due***; look at and pay attention to those entitled to respect; honor to those entitled to honor. 8.* **Leave no debt unpaid, except the debt of love to others: for he who loves his neighbor has done what the law demands.** (Romans 13:7-8 EDNT)

Recently, I had to use Mother's Reserve for a special need and it left me without pocket money for daily needs. But God knew my needs. Here is what happened: needing $122 pocket money for doctor's copay, etc., I stopped by my rural mailbox. There was an Insurance check for $81 for over payment; then I went by Walmart to pick up my new glasses and was given $70 for an overcharge. This totaled $151, when I only needed $122. God is good! There's more: I had loaned $100 which I did not expect back, but it was handed to me the same day. I had "**enough and then some**," God is good!

The Ten Percent Rule

Could it be that the Children's Bread is made more useful by divine coinage values? Since tithe was a Tenth of income and that supported the Temple and the Priests, could there be a 10% rule on purchases as well. When you find a bargain is it at some other person's loss? Could it be the wealth of the wicked being stored away for the righteous? I have built churches and schools using the 10% rule. One example I will share: a faculty member who by my standard was wealthy, asked that the school buy for his campus apartment a La-Z-Boy chair because of sleeping difficulties. Searching all over Chattanooga for a bargain, none could be found. The best price was $450 but the chair seemed weak for a 300-pound man, so I decided against the purchase. Taking a back road on the way back to campus, there was a yard sale going on. Stopping to see, there was a top of the line leather La-Z-Boy recliner in the yard. Asking, *"Is this chair for sale?"* the response, *"Yes, if you will take it right now, the price is $45.* "There was my 10% rule, but not on the cheapest, but on the top of the line. God works in mysterious ways to perform wonders for His people. Somehow, we just do not see financial things the way God does! What happened to faith, **the substance of things hoped for and evidence of things not seen?** (Hebrews 11)

Silence Facing Selfishness

It appears the rich have more than "enough" and should share their extra resources generously with the needy. However, personal selfishness and greediness causes some to hold on to funds that are needed for Kingdom work. This is the concept of paying it forward; not putting away for a rainy day or to accumulate personal wealth or to increase personal standing among peers. There is clear guidance from Jesus for those who have more than "enough" resources needed to support personal and family needs: share with the poor and follow Him. Jesus suggested that some had strayed from the right path and should take steps to follow the plan and "come back" to true Kingdom discipleship; however, when the offer to participate is refused or neglected, Jesus simply remained "silent" and permitted the man to walk away from an opportunity to participate in the Kingdom. Through selfishness the young man missed the "more blessed" aspects of wealth sharing!

> *One thing you lack: go sell your possessions and give the funds to the poor and you shall have treasure in heaven:* and come back and follow Me. 22. And he was depressed at the request and went away with great sadness: for he had much property. *(And Jesus let him go!)* (Mark 10:21, 22 EDNT)

A Word of Warning

The purpose of wealth is made clear in the writing of James. He observed that needed funds had long been kept from the poor and had become corroded. The gold and silver of the New Testament era were not pure and could easily corrode. Just as fine cloths stored improperly may become moth eaten and corrosion will damage or destroy stockpiled metal, so the hoarding of wealth dishonors the Divine plan for the use of material resources.

> 2. Corruption has fallen on your wealth and your fine clothes are food for moths. 3. *Your gold and silver are corroded and made septic by rust; and the decay is proof to you of how worthless your coins are.* It is a canker which will consume your family tree like fire. These are your last days and you spent them storing up a personal fortune for an undesirable

outcome, 4. you have kept back the pay of the reapers
who worked your land, and the great number of men
in the Lord's army has heard their cries against you.
God listened to their complaint. (James 5:2-4 EDNT)

Need for Dissembling

An instance that illustrates the need for dissembling the structured outreach agenda happened when Philip of the Jerusalem church listened to and obeyed an Angle of the Lord. On a walk in the desert, Philip found a man seated in a chariot reading the scroll of Isaiah. He joined himself to the situation and asked, "Do you understand what you are reading?" The clear answer, "How can I unless someone explains this to me? Was the prophet speaking of himself or someone else?" And at that time and place using the same scripture, Philip explained the good news to the man from Ethiopia. When the stranger from another culture understood, he believed and requested initiation through baptism. Philip made sure of his active faith, baptized a convert and the Ethiopian carried the Christian message back to his homeland (Acts 8:26-39). This was not an institutionalized program; it was personal action at the direction of the Spirit. Such behavior will break down the over programming and disassemble the structured outreach and permit individuals to participate in making disciples and advancing the kingdom. More believers must give the gift of self and an offering of time to the Cause of Christ. *A gift opens the way and ushers the giver into the presence of great men.* (Proverbs 18:16 NIV)

X

Participating
In Kingdom Support

Individual and Institutional Narrowing

A process called "individual narrowing" occurs
in the lives of most people. As one ages, activities
that are not done well or enjoyed are eliminated.
Consequently, a narrow view of life develops and
the ability to see broader possibilities is limited. This
limitation is often projected to the social groups
in which they participate. As the family and/or
congregations age the same process occurs. With
almost no flexibility, the group ends up in a straitjacket
of problematic behavior that over utilizes available
time and energy and limits outreach to others outside
the family, community or congregation. It is up to
the maturing constituency to disassemble the well-
meaning but unworkable activities and introduce a
more aggressive initiative to broaden the base of
operations and the lifestyle necessary to fulfill Jesus'
Challenge "*As you go make disciples.*"

A Generic Blindness

My six-decade attempt to support faith-based
operations at a personal and a congregational level

required a generic blindness to the sectarian nature of local faith-based centers of worship and provided a less biased framework for social research related to the barrier walls caused by failure of lifestyle behavior by professing believers. The effort to understand faith groups as social-based institutions and develop an appreciation for a Faith-based heritage enhanced my personal spiritual life and provided a basis for continued social research.

Causes for Sectarian Divisions

Most faith-based divisions can be traced to cultural roots, national origins or the ego of a few. Jude wrote about those who caused separations and divisions because they were natural men without the Spirit.

> *17. But, beloved, you must remember the words once spoken before of the apostles of our Lord Jesus Christ; 18. how they told you there should be ridiculing spirits in the last time, who would make their ungodly appetites into a rule of life. 19. **Such are the men who now keep themselves apart; fleshly creatures without the Spirit.** 20. It is for you, beloved, to make your most holy faith the foundation of your lives, and to go on praying in the power of the Holy Spirit; 21. Maintain yourselves in the love of God, and wait for the mercy of our Lord Jesus Christ, with eternal life as your goal.* (Jude 1:17-21 EDNT)

> Paul also wrote about this issue: *12. We have not received the spirit of the world, but the Spirit that is of God; that we might know the things that are freely given to us by God. 13. We do not speak of these things in language taught by men, but that which*

*the Holy Spirit teaches; explaining spiritual things
in spiritual words. 14.* **The natural man does not
accept the things of the Spirit of God: for they are
nonsense to him: they just do not make sense to
him: neither can he understand them, because
they are only discerned spiritual**ly. *15. But the man
with spiritual insight can judge the worth of everything,
yet no one can give an informed judgment of him.
16. For who knows the mind of the Lord, that he
may instruct him? But we have the mind of Christ.* (1
Corinthians 2:12-16 EDNT)

Antecedent Causes

My search for antecedent causes for sectarian
divisions took me into every region of the United
States and required extensive travel in forty-six (46)
countries. Research was directed toward the social
and cultural foundations of sectarian groups. The
problem of negative participation in religious worship
has created declining attendance, as well as the
destructive aspects of personal mental reservation
to commitment and blatant disagreement with
sound tenets of faith. Taking a seat at the table is
an opportunity for participation not taking a side or a
position for or against something.

In an effort to understand the sectarian
view, extensive research was done on the oldest
Pentecostal group and the largest Protestant group
in America. Doctorates in Theology, Philosophy,
and Education were earned during this search.
Meanwhile, my schedule was filled with teaching,
academic administration, research and writing, but
colleagues and friends have encouraged sequels to

my best-known works. My last twenty (20+) books were an attempt to follow that prompt.

- ***Why Churches Die***. *(1972; 2007) ISBN* **978-1-9796019-03** A fresh assessment of congregational vitality to determine thirty-five reasons why faith-based congregations were losing their pristine power of outreach.

- ***Interpreting an Author's Words***. *(2008)* **ISBN 978-0980-164-74**—Define both formal and informal study and writing skills by understanding how to clearly interpret the spoken and written words of others.

- ***Titanic Lesson***. *(2008) ISBN* **978-0-9796019-6-5** -An answer to the question: "Do historic realities predict problems for a growing faith-based group?

- ***Sympathetic Leadership Cybernetics***. *(2010)* **ISBN 978-1-9354345-28** – This work attempts to clarify management and leadership in the context of organizational and institutional functionality and charts a course for organizations to serve the needs of people through shepherd management and servant leadership.

- ***Why Christianity Fails in America***. (2010) **ISBN 978-0-9796019-10**-- A call for an internal redirection of the heart and soul to make the pristine faith viable in the Twenty-first century.

- ***How to Build a Better Spouse Trap***. *(2010)* **ISBN 978-1—9354344-50** – A major failure of faith-based groups is they have made little difference in the lives of individuals and their function in the family. How to choose a mate, learn for our mistakes, stay married, and teach others to break the cycle of dysfunctional relationships. The family unit is a microcosm of faith-based behavior.

- ***Discipleship.*** *(2010) ISBN* **978-0-9796019-5-8**--A revived edition to better explain the process of a believer's lifestyle from conversion (change direction), to discipleship (learning), to apostle (mature enough to be trusted with the message of grace.)

- ***SO TALES.*** *(2011)* **ISBN 978-1-9354345-80** -- Preserving true 240 true stories from the past for the benefit of family and friends.

- ***Designing Valid Research.*** *(2011)* **ISBN 978-1-9354345-73** – A guide to designing a research proposal and developing a social scientific dissertation.

- ***Titanic Lessons.*** *(2012)* **ISBN 978-0-9796019-6-5** – An effort to demonstrate that bigger is not necessarily better and that all building of machines, organizations, and institutions must use material that meets the precise requirements of the task. This must be applied to people, process, and functionality of the human element and the mechanics must match the environment.

- ***Why Wait Till Sunday?*** (2012) **ISBN 978-1-935434-27-6**-- A renewal plan for older congregations who depended on programs coming down from sectarian authority rather than locally generated ideas and involvement in seven (7) aspects of renewal.

- ***Fighting the Amalekites.*** *(2013)* **ISBN 978-1-935434-30-6** – The unhealthy addictions, unproductive habits, an uncontrolled tongue are all little "Amalekites" unless these are destroyed they will become the destroyer. These join the Amalekites that ambush and take advantage of spiritual weaknesses.

- ***Remedial and Surrogate Parenting*** *(2013)* **ISBN 978-1-9354344-81**--Children are a gift of God and a legacy of faith-based families; therefore, parenting skills are an essential aspect of religion. This work is guidance for remedial human development (0-20) for parents, teachers, and childcare workers.

- ***The EVERGREEN Devotional New Testament – C.A.F.E. Edition.*** *(2013, 2017)* **ISBN 978-1-9354342-69** – *EDNT is a* 42-year project to translate common NT Greek and determine the meaning "then" and how words can best be expressed "now" and remain true to the original intent expressed in a common devotional language.

- ***Transformational Leadership in Education.*** *(2013) Second Edition ISBN* **978-1-9354342-38**-- *A* strengths-based approach to education for administrators, teachers, and guidance counselors.

- ***Tear Down These Walls.*** (2013) **ISBN 978-1-9354341-84** -- A priority agenda must be to make people moral citizens of the world before they can become mystical citizens of heaven. Where organized groups choose not to function, personal action could make a difference and break down some of the barriers that divide the faith-based community and strengthen the "One Lord-One Faith–One Baptism" message.

- ***Recycled Words n' Stuff.*** *(2016)* ISBN **978-1-9354348-63** – A collection of short narratives and essays of general interest.

- ***The Children's Bread*** *–Unlocking Whole Life Stewardship by Accessing Kingdom Economics* *and Personal Wealth* (2018) **ISBN 978-1-935434-90-0**.

- ***Kingdom Growth Through Missional Behavior*** *-Growing a Relational Congregation (2019)* **ISBN 97 8-1-935434-91-7**-- *Advancing spiritual formation for congregational vitality and missional lifestyle.*

- ***Research Methods for Problem Solvers and Critical Thinkers.*** *(2019)* **ISBN 978-1-935434-92-4**– Guidance in development a Master's thesis, designing a doctoral research proposal and constructing a defendable dissertation based on social scientific research with an objective of positive social change.

Missional Reality

All believers are called to a missionary endeavor and are chosen for a specific task. They must leave their comfort zone, make preparation to enter a strange and hostile world and develop a capacity to see every person and situation as an opportunity for both social and spiritual advancement. They must function within a limited budget, with a minimum of equipment and tools to facilitate their work and must cut corners at every opportunity to stretch their financial resources to the furthest extent. Normally, they become responsible, through deputation, to raise funds to replace what was used in order to continue their spiritual journey of making disciples as they travel. This is true "Lifestyle missions." Then when they achieve a certain level of learning, they must work even harder to teach them all the Jesus did and taught and guide them to become a functioning believer with a moral and ethical lifestyle. This process may mean separation from extended family, friends, and the comforts with which they had become accustomed and venturing into a harsh and unfriendly world. All believers were saved to serve not just occupy a seat at worship services. Taking a seat at the Lord's Table and receiving the children's bread enables them to daily work at "making disciples" as a normal part of their Christian lifestyle.

> *1. This is a faithful saying, if a man desire leadership oversight, he is aspiring to a noble task. 2. One holding an office of watchful care must **be** scrupulous, faithful to one wife, watchful, sensible, orderly, hospitable, experienced in teaching; 3. Neither **be** intemperate, nor quarrelsome, free from the love of money; but gentle, not contentious, not a craving for possessions; 4. He must **be** one who is a good head of his own family, and keeps his children in order by winning their full respect; 5. If a man has not learned how to manage his own household, will he know how to govern God's church? 6. Not a recent convert, lest being puffed up and fall into judgment of the devil. 7. Moreover he must **have** a good report from those outside the church; that he not fall into reproach and into the snare of the devil.* (1 Timothy 3:1-7 EDNT)

Lifestyle of Complete Obedience

To think and behave in a missional sense is a lifestyle of complete obedience to the Believers Challenge in Matthew 28:16-20. All believers are in full time Christian service regardless of how they earn their living. Serving others is not about one's occupation; it is about a relationship with Jesus and the cause of His kingdom on earth. However, those taking a seat at the *"making disciples"* table must develop a missional lifestyle. A believer, functioning with a missionary-mindset, must first develop a moral and ethical lifestyle, be grounded in the Word, and develop an unselfish and positive attitude toward life and living. One must become a moral citizen of the world before they can be accepted as a missional leader or become a mystical citizen of heaven. To become involved in the missional aspects of Kingdom service, a believer must maintain a *"present tense"* relationship with God and be in true fellowship with other believers. Scripture is clear, believers must meet the scriptural standard and *"be"* and maintain certain standards. Living a missional lifestyle is certainly a present tense reality.

> *4. Let every man test himself for innocence, and then he shall rejoice in himself and not in another. 5. For every man must carry his own personal load. 6. Let him who receives instructions in the word share in support of the teacher's living. 7. Be not deceived; no man can snub God:* **for whatever, a man may sow this also he will reap; 8. For he who plants proceeds in the field of the flesh shall have a spoiled harvest; but he who plants proceeds in the field of the Spirit shall harvest life everlasting. 9. And let us not become weary in doing what is right: for if we do not weaken our resolve, in due season we will collect the good harvest.** *10. As we have opportunity, let us practice generosity to all, especially to those who are of the household of faith.* (Galatians 6:4-10 EDNT)

Believers Present Tense Lifestyle

To be effective as a believer, one must remain current in faith and practice. This must be demonstrated consistently and constantly in a present tense lifestyle to support a believer's witness. Any weakness in lifestyle-behavior will weaken their witness and usefulness. Present tense is used to describe habits, unchanging situations, general truths, and fixed arrangements. **Present tense** predominantly expresses a current event or state of being and describes what is true, what occurs, what is habitual or characteristic of behavior. God has factored into Faith-based living the ways and means to maintain a current lifestyle: confession, conversion, conduct, celebration, collect, communion, challenge, and consensus.

1. **CONFESSION** – acknowledgment of human weakness and the need for forgiveness. (1 John 1:5-10)

2. **CONVERSION** – a transformation in which one adopts a new lifestyle. (2 Corinthians 5:17-21; 2 Peter 3:9)

3. **CONDUCT** – personal appearance, behavior and demeanor (Ephesians 5:1-29)

4. **CELEBRATION** – remembering the source of salvation, honoring the "worth-ship" of God in all of life, taking a seat at the Lord's Table, and acknowledging Divine leadership. There should be prayer, reading of scripture, and instruction in the Word. (Romans 12:1-21)

5. **COLLECT** – regular worship that includes a collective gathering of congregational needs that brings improved lifestyle. (Hebrews 10:22-15)

6. **COMMUNION** – regularly participate in the Lord's Supper (Eucharist) to remember the Lord's death until He returns. (1 Corinthians 11:23-33)

7. **CHALLENGE** – listen to the Believer's Challenge from Jesus and behave "as you go make disciples," baptize and teach converts to observe all that Jesus taught. (Matthew 28:18-20; Mark 16:19-20}

8. **CONSENSUS** – the congregation should function by consensus "it seemed good to us and the Holy Spirit being assembled in one accord." (Acts 1:22-29)

*25. it seemed good, being assembled with one accord, to send chosen men to you with our beloved Barnabas and Paul; 26. men who have risked their lives for the name of the Lord Jesus Christ. 27. We have sent Judas and Silas, who shall confirm this message by their words. 28. For it seemed good to the Holy Spirit and to us, not to impose any extra burden on you, apart from the necessary ones: 2***9. that you abstain from food sacrificed to idols, from tasting blood, from things strangled, and from sexual immorality***: if you guard against these things, you will be doing right. Be strong! (Acts 15:25-29 EDNT)*

A Common Agenda

One Faith-based group will never produce world peace or feed the children or care for the sick and dying. One group cannot eliminate poverty, violence, drugs, human trafficking or complete global moral change. Although this is not essential to Divine redemption; correcting the moral corruption certainly opens the way for a move of the Spirit. There must be a renewal of the Spirit of pristine believers to facilitate a common agenda and make people moral citizens of the world before we attempt to make into mystical citizens of heaven. Positive social change certainly does expedite spiritual renewal. Synergetic cooperation is not to suggest a least common denominator dogma or that all Faith-based peoples must join into one body, because individuals do not have to go outside their culture or compromise their sacred reality to work together for the good of mankind. Culture and tradition are social glue that holds people of faith together. Jews did not have to deny Judaism or Gentiles follow the Hebrew culture. This cultural bonding is strong, but compromise (*a "together-promise" agreement*) is a necessary part of the way forward that leaves no one behind. The Jewish Council in Jerusalem wrote to Gentile converts to give up those practices that would draw them back to their old lifestyle.

No Discharge in the War

There should be no intentional delay in advancing the gospel. R and R (rest and recreation) Furloughs may exist, but there is no discharge in this spiritual warfare to "*gospelize*" the world. Opportunity equals obligation. James was clear about missed opportunities: ***17. Therefore if a man has the power to do good; and fails to do good it is sinful.*** *(James 4:17 EDNT)* When God opens a door, believers must *"Strick while the iron is hot "* or *"work while it is day for* *the night comes when no man can work,"* or the words of an old farmer when the field hands were working too slowly, *"Keep working, you are burning daylight."* Often, we do not properly see the light of each day as an opportunity to labor in the Lord's vineyard.

Wear the Complete Armor

Putting on the clothes of a believer is not enough, we must "**wear the whole armor of God**" and be a good soldier. Paul told young Timothy, *"Join the ranks of those who share hardships as a soldier of Jesus Christ. 4. No active warrior entangles himself with ordinary affairs; so he may please the one who enlisted him as a soldier." (2 Timothy 2:5-7 EDNT)*

> *10. Finally, my brothers, be strengthened in the Lord, and in the power of his unlimited resource. 11. **Wear the complete armor of God**, so you can stand against the strategy and assault of the adversary. 12. For our wrestling is not against a physical enemy, but against evil princes of darkness who rule this world, against hosts of spiritual wickedness in heavenly warfare. 13. Wherefore **wear the complete armor of God that you may be able to withstand evil attacks when they come and be found still standing.** 14. Stand your ground, being protected by truth, and having integrity for a breastplate; 15. and the gospel of peace preparing your feet for battle, 16. Above all, take the shield of faith to extinguish all the fiery darts of the wicked. 17. And take the helmet which is salvation, and the sword of the Spirit, which is the word of God: 18. **Praying on every occasion, through petition in the Spirit, with vigilant and unwearied and supplication for all saints;** 19. and pray for me, that fluency of speech may be given*

*me, that I may make known courageously the sacred
secret of the gospel, 20. for which I am an envoy in
a coupling-chain bound to a guard: that in spite of
that detail I may speak bravely, as I ought to speak.*
(Ephesians 6:10-20 EDNT)

The Secular Prophets were Wrong

None of these secular prophets were correct.
The predictions concerning the early demise of
personal faith were premature. God is not dead! Faith
in God did not fade away as an old soldier. Friedrich
Nietzsche's 1882 calculation about the early decline
in faith-based worship was wrong. Both Bernard
Shaw and H. G. Wells predicted an end to what they
called the *"religious phase"* of history; they were
wrong. Even as late as mid-century, Julian Huxley
wrote about *"God's last fading smile"* and compared
it to the grin of a Cheshire cat. Although attendance
at religious meetings has declined, a basic belief in
God remains deep in the human psychic. What is
lacking is the dynamic faith that makes life a shared
journey with God and others. Missing is a genuine
togetherness and moral agreement concerning the
faith once delivered by the saints. (Jude 1:3)

Must Remove Barriers

Where organized groups choose not to function,
personal action can make a difference and break
down some of the barriers to an action agenda that
could strengthen the One Lord-One Faith message.
Perhaps, a better missional "second front" in the
global spiritual battle or a strategic "guerilla warfare"
of believers with a missional lifestyle could make a

difference. Remember, the goal for a global outreach is not domination or control, but emancipation from poverty and violence and liberty to choose a personal and eternal destiny in the hands of Providence. For this to happen, the barriers to personal faith and action must be removed.

Second Front and Guerilla Warfare

A generic least common denominator creed is not the answer, there must a re-energized approach to faith-based operations on three fronts: fervent local worship groups, eager "second front" outreach units, and strategic "guerilla warfare" activity behind the lines to teach the teachable and reach the reachable. No one faith group has been able to reach all the population of the world. In fact, all the major Faith-based groups have divisions that limit their global effectiveness. Each group behaving as if they have found the "Holy Grail" and have exclusive access to the "secrets" of eternal redemption.

Little Common Ground

Tragically, there is little common ground; however, moral leadership must start somewhere and seek to make a difference in the world. Provided the hostility and rivalry can be adjusted, gates in the dividing walls opened, and a common cause becomes self-evident, there is hope for a moral and faith-based agenda that can change the world one person at a time. This common ground must be faith-based and known to be true without ecclesiastical validation. The personal expression of faith is essential to this process. And there must be a full understanding of Bible-based teaching on economics and wealth. God uses people, but people need funds to support their families and their mission to the lost. This is also required for Kingdom Economics to work and for Personal Wealth to be acquired and released to advance Kingdom work. Otherwise, there will never be sufficient funds to advance the Message of Grace to fulfill John's statement *"For God so loved the world that He gave His only begotten Son, that whoever believes in Him should not perish, but have everlasting life."*

Differences Divide Commonalities Advance

Differences divide and camouflage commonalities that could bring unity of effort in overcoming basic problems that must be solved to advance the gospel and meet basic human needs. The concern for food, shelter, safety of family, spiritual redemption, and world peace should be the common goal of all who claim to honor and worship *the one and only God, Creator and Sustainer of the Universe*. It is self-evident that all who serve one God should be working together to provide for the necessities and nourishment of all His creation. This would require finding common ground and advancing a common cause to benefit all the People of God: this would restore meaning to "One Lord-One Faith-One Baptism" in the world. Since this is what God requires and the sacred founders of monotheistic faith requested, the selfishness of the human element should not be allowed to hinder this righteous cause.

Viable Faith-based Worship

The only hope for a viable monotheistic, faith-based worship and witness is an internal redirection of the heart and soul that brings with it a moral lifestyle and personal protest against the immorality of society. Such redirection will bring both a commitment to the cardinal tenets of sacred writings and a spirit of cooperation and teamwork among people. Such a change could free sufficient funds to accomplish a unified task; however, if Faith-based groups continue to operate their own "dog and pony show" there is little hope for world evangelism. This change in the standard "religious rhetoric" could break the barriers of "freeze framed thinking," and "name brand religion" and make One Lord and One Faith meaningful again. According to sacred writings:

> The words of the Psalmist David: **Behold, how good and pleasant it is when brothers dwell in unity!** (Psalms 133:1); the words of Jesus: **"A kingdom divided is brought to destruction; and a house divided falls."** (Luke 11:17 EDNT); the words of the Quran: **Let there arise out of you one community, inviting to all that is good, enjoining what is right, and forbidding what is wrong: those will be prosperous. Be not like those who are divided amongst themselves and fall into disputations after receiving clear signs: for them is a dreadful penalty.** (Qur'an 3:105)

Stewardship is a matter of the heart.
Possessions often interfere with the
relationship with God by steering one away
from spiritual matters. Wealth brings
benefits, but everyone must be aware of the
power of money to lure one away from the
right path and the blessings of God.

XI

Growing In Faith-Based Stewardship

Giving vs. Receiving

Why is it more blessed to give than to receive? Why is this idea the most unbelieved beatitude of the Bible? (Acts 20:35) The ability to give means one has "more than enough" to support the family and the basic obligations of life. Out of the overage of "more than enough" the giver feels blessed to share with others the true blessings of God and hard work.

> *31. Therefore, be on guard and remember that for the space of three years I never stopped warning you night and day with tears. 32. And now, brethren, I commend you to God, and to the word of His grace, which is able to make you strong, **and give you an inheritance among the consecrated ones**. 33. I have never asked for silver or gold or clothing from anyone. 34. You have seen yourself that **these hands have supplied not only my own needs, but for the people with me.** 35. In all things, I gave you an example of working hard and that one must provide for the poor. **Remember the words of the Lord Jesus, when He said, It is more blessed to give than to receive.** 36. When he had finished speaking, he knelt and prayed with them. (Acts 20:28-38 EDNT)*

Disgraceful Teaching

It is disgraceful that the "gold, glory, and glamour" teaching of some has caused many to ignore the pathway of spiritual economics to seek materialistic success instead of the divine route to "enough" to support the family with "more than enough" overage to further support others and kingdom work. Paul was the supreme example of a self-supporting ministry, when he, through his personal labor in *"tent making,"* supported himself and his ministry team. This is a prime example of a by-vocational ministry who generated *"enough and then some"* to support himself and those who traveled with him. The example of clergy today seeking personal wealth at the expense of the kingdom is disgraceful!

> *17. **The time is ripe for judgment to begin with God's house: and if our turn comes first, what will be the end of those that disobey the gospel of God?*** (1 Peter 4:17 EDNT)

> *I have a charge to give to my fellow seniors among you: 2. **be shepherds to the flock God has given you, do your watchful care, not out of an obligation, but willingly; not for gain, but freely; 3. Not as a noble with an inherited estate, but setting an example to the congregation.*** (1 Peter 5:1-3 EDNT)

The Ancient Meaning of Wealth

Sacred scripture explains wealth in terms of property, possessions, and productivity in the context of fields, farming, or a rural agrarian culture. The economy was based on a social philosophy showing the advantage of a simple rural life as compared to the complexity of urban society. During this period of history, a simple rural life was valued as better than an aristocratic or city life. The production and maintaining of crops, flocks and herds of animals made one self-sufficient while the fragmented urban lifestyle destroyed personal dignity, create weakness and alienated people. It was believed that the cultivation of the soil had a spiritual nature closer to God who created order out of confusion.

Daniel and his Hebrew friends (Daniel 1:8) lived by a simple truism in refusing the kings meat and wine, which was against their God and personal health. Consequently, they asked for a comparative study with the Hebrews eating only vegetables and drinking water while the other young men ate the kings mean and drank wine. There is a warning in scripture to exercise self-control when you are being lured into a scheme to get rich. *"Better is a little with righteousness, than vast revenues without justice."* (Proverbs 16:8) Rather than seeking the wealth of the world, have a little more faith and seek first the kingdom of God.

> *Have a little more faith. 29. And seek not what you shall eat, or drink, neither be disturbed with cares. 30. For all these things do the nations of the world seek after: and your Father knows that you need these things, 31.* ***But rather seek the kingdom of God and all these things shall be added to you.*** *32. Fear not, little flock; for it is your Father's good pleasure to give you the kingdom. 33.* ***Keep your assets liquid and give alms; provide yourselves a purse that does***

not grow old, a treasure in the heavens that fails not, where no thief has access, neither moths can spoil. 34. For where your treasure is, there your heart will be also. (Luke 12:28-34 EDNT)

Wealth is not Limited to Money

Scripture records several as being wealthy: Abraham, Job, Joseph, and Solomon. The Bible is not in conflict with wealth, but is simply concerned that mankind view prosperity from God's perspective. Wealth is not limited to money or the numerical value of coinage; it is based on "value added" placed on resources with reference to the sweat equity, the cost to the laborer, and its spiritual value to assist the poor and support kingdom endeavors. There is a spiritual dimension to evaluating wealth; one who enjoys God's blessings is rich beyond measure when compared to one who rejects God's call to repentance and the free gift of salvation. In one case the poor man has **extraordinary** blessings from God and the rich man is impoverished in spirit and soul and their material goods are fleeting. God is the source of prosperity in any form. (1 Chronicles 29:12) Man is unable to gain wealth without the generosity of God.

> *12. Blood-related* and fortunate is the man who flinches not under the enticement of testing: for when he is proved trustworthy, he shall be given the wreath of honor that verifies vitality, which God promised to all who worship out of a benevolent heart. 13. Let no man say when he is enticed, God allured me to evil: for God does not use wickedness to validate the trustworthiness of any man. 14. But every man is attracted to wicked deeds, when he chooses action*

based on personal desire, and hope of pleasure. 15. Then when personal desire has joined together with enticement, it produces a voluntary transgression: and this offense produces separation from observant morality, and at the end separation from God. 16. **Do not wander from the right or deviate from the true course, my cherished band of brothers. 17. Every unspoiled and true benefaction is from above, and comes down from the Father of all light, with whom there is no changeableness, neither a dark side where there is no light.** *18. Of his own determination procreated as a Father all of us with the expression of genuineness, that we should be the first matured and collected fruit of God's created beings.* (James 1:12-18 EDNT)

* v12 to bless, in Middle English used at the time of KJV, had a meaning related to "blood" used to consecrate an altar; thus, the use of "blood-related."

*17. You may say, My power and the strength of my hands have produced this wealth. 18. But remember the LORD your God, for it is He who gives you the ability to produce wealth, and this confirms His covenant, which He swore to your ancestors, and confirms today. (*Deuteronomy 8:17,18 EDOT)

Prosperity comes from the Hand of God

Prosperity is comprehensive, all-encompassing and comes from the Hand of God. The definition of "prosperity" is not all about money; the concept of prosperity is a comprehensive assortment of good things and money is only one factor. However, one must always remember whether one is rich or poor God's blessings are available. The limiting factor is based on attitude, a predisposition to act, and motive:

the reason or purpose for action. The Bible does not promise that being a follower of Jesus will make one wealthy. Being rich is not a sign of God's favor, but poverty is a natural consequence of poor judgment and foolish actions.

> *9 To the discerning all of them are right; they are upright to those who have found knowledge. 10 Choose my instruction instead of silver, knowledge rather than choice gold, 11 for wisdom is more precious than rubies,* (Proverbs 8:9-11 NIV); *13 Do not love sleep or you will grow poor; stay awake and you will have food to spare. 14 "It's no good, it's no good!" says the buyer-- then goes off and boasts about the purchase. 15 Gold there is, and rubies in abundance, but lips that speak knowledge are a rare jewel.* (Job 8:13-15 NIV); *27 The human spirit is[a] the lamp of the LORD that sheds light on one's inmost being. 21 for drunkards and gluttons become poor, and drowsiness clothes them in rags.* (Proverbs 23:21 NIV)

Spiritual Arithmetic

The wise man Solomon understood spiritual arithmetic and wrote *"Two are better than one because they have a good reward for their labor."* (Ecclesiastes 4:9-12) Working together is normally better than working alone; working together with God is the most beneficial way for all concerned.   Moses, according to the Hebrew Bible and the Qur'an, was a religious leader, lawgiver and prophet, to whom the authorship of the Torah is attributed. Deep in these ancient writings were the laws about obedience that told God's People, *"Then I will give peace in the land, and you shall lie down, and none shall make you afraid: and five of you shall chase a hundred, and a hundred of you shall put ten thousand to flight.* (Leviticus 26:1-12) Yet numbers are not the issue.

A Few Good Men Plus God

In the Book of Judges (7:1-28) there is a record of Gideon, who reduced his band of soldiers to a small troupe of 300 and gained full victory over a great army. Gideon began with 32,000 men but reduced the number to 10,000; still it was too many for God to receive credit for victory. Spiritual counting may be different from mathematical calculation, because spiritual counting is based on what a *"few good men"* with sincere commitment and divine guidance could do, when the masses depend on their strength instead of God's power. Progress could be made by exposing the general public to the unlimited power of God rather than the restrictive sectarian positions that basically deny foundational biblical principles. When individuals refuse to walk on the foundation stones that mark the Right Path, there is little benefit or security on the road ahead for family, friends, or Faith-based congregation.

Blessed, not Forsaken

The righteous are not forsaken or required to beg for the scraps that fall from the Master's Table, but are blessed with blood-bought added values in their daily transactions. The energy exerted in Faith-based living and service is channeled back to meet their needs. Since in human economics, energy may be traded for money, by exchanging work for funds. In Kingdom

Economics God uses good and valued conversion rates when believers exchange physical labor (sweat equity) for funds to operate their family, assist the poor, and support places and leaders of worship. This makes volunteerism the best paid position in God's work. Why? God always blesses busy hands! Sweat equity is a valued added interest to physical work.

> *2* I will go before you and will level the mountains; I will break down gates of bronze and cut through bars of iron. *3 **I will give you hidden treasures, riches stored in secret places, so that you may know that I am the LORD,** the God of Israel, who summons you by name.* (Isaiah 45:2-3 NIV)

Volunteer Labor has Coinage Value

However, most Faith-based entities do not know how to appreciate or count volunteer labor in their budget or audit. The poor do not appreciate small or incremental accumulation of small change. When I lived in Jacksonville, FL, a friend of mine started a small company and then sold it for a $7,000,000 profit. I picked him up at the airport for a visit and as we came to the toll bridge where I was about to toss a quartet, he instructed me to go through the booth where I could get a receipt. I was shocked that a man who had millions would be concerned about a 25-cent receipt. In discussion, he said, *"**That is why you are poor, and I am rich**. You don't think about the little things. There are four toll booths from the airport to your home and a roundtrip would be eight (8) quarters; that's $2.00 and that means $2.00* *income that would have been lost without the wisdom of saving receipts."*

Civil and Religious Leaders working Together

The Temple was being rebuilt in Zechariah (4:1) and the Prophet wrote, *"Do not despise these small beginnings, for the Lord rejoices to see the work begin, to see the plum line in Zerubbabel's hand." The angel had said, to Zerubbabel, "Not by* **might** *(wealth), nor by* **power**, *but by my* **spirit** *(breath), says the Lord of hosts."* It appears from the Hebrew text that it is the "poor" who despise or "look down on" the day of small things. Even a small beginning was an encouragement to Zerubbabel, the **civil** leader and Joshua, the **religious** leader in rebuilding the walls of the Lord's house.

> God spoke to Solomon and said, *"**Ask for whatever you want me to give you**." 8* Solomon answered God, "You have shown great kindness to David my father and have made me king in his place. *9* Now, LORD God, let your promise to my father David be confirmed, for you have made me king over a people who are as *numerous as the dust of the earth. 10 Give me* **wisdom and knowledge, that I may lead this people**, *for who is able to govern this great people of yours?" 11* God said to Solomon, *"**Since this is your heart's desire and you have not asked for wealth, possessions or honor, nor for the death of your enemies, and since you have not asked for a long life but for wisdom and knowledge to govern my** people over whom I have made you king, 12* therefore wisdom and knowledge will be given you. And I will also give you wealth, possessions and honor, *such as*

no king who was before you ever had and none after you will have." (2 Chronicles 1:11 NIV)

Value Added by the Master

Most have heard the story of the old violin being sold at auction. The bids were small until an old Master picked up the historic violin and began to play. The bids went up and up as people understood the value added by the Master Violinist. So, it is with God's economics; it is a value-added plan. The concept that *"Little is much when God is in it!"* is based on Micah 5:2 and Matthew 14:17.

In the harvest field now ripened
There's a work for all to do;
Hark! The voice of God is calling
To the harvest - calling you.
Little is much when God is in it!
Labor not for wealth or fame.
There's a crown and you can win it,
If you go in Jesus' Name.
Does the place you're called to labor
Seem too small and little known?
It is great if God is in it,
And He'll not forget His own.

- Kittie Louise Suffield (1884-1972)

These lyrics enlarge the meaning of the concept: *"We have here only five loaves of bread and two fish."* This was "enough and then some," the boy's mother had packed more than enough for his lunch. The "extra" was available and Jesus could use a small packed lunch as an asset to advance the Kingdom with much left over. Why only twelve baskets full: there were only 12 disciples with one basket each. God work is only limited by laborers and God's blessings. Little is much when God is involved.

Nonprofit Accounting

Most Faith-based operations around the world are run by volunteer labor. Normally, the volunteer workers are underappreciated because a value is not clearly established for their labor. Remember:

*18. For scripture says, **You shall not muzzle the ox treading out the corn. And, the laborer is worthy of his compensation.*** (1 Timothy 5:17-18 EDNT)

The Federal IRS permits the actual value of voluntary labor to be booked as a donation to nonprofit organizations. If it cost the church $300 to fix a plumbing problem and a volunteer did the work, a simple *"Thank you"* is not sufficient accounting for the labor. Nonprofit Accounting Regulations and the IRS permit a non-for-profit group to book the *"value received"* in their accounting and audit and provide a donation receipt to the volunteer for their labor which they may count as a donation on their tax return. This is using Kingdom Economics to physically and financially support Faith-based labor, budgets and income. [See Appendix A for more data]

A Stipulated Settlement

Some years ago, my wife slipped on ice and had a bad fall. After treatment and evaluation, she received a Worker's Comp settlement for 35%

permanent disability and a stipulated settlement. We asked that the compensation be divided into monthly payments until she reached 62 and would be eligible for Social Security. The month she turned 62, the checks stopped, naturally she could not work, and dependence had developed on the monthly check. But that is not the end of the story: without knowledge of the situation or the need, a Christian businessman in another country, who hardly knew my wife, started sending her monthly the exact same amount as the previous Worker's Compensation stipend. This has continued monthly for the past nine (9) years. God is good!

Another case is my ministry through education income is similar. As a retired pastor and professor who worked for missionary-type salary, at age 80 plus, income was limited. When a writing consultant contract that netted $500 per month ended abruptly due to an economic situation, there was reason for concern. Naturally, it was needed funds and the loss would cripple the cash flow of my ongoing ministry through education. Without this knowledge, a couple, to whom I had ministered in the past, decide to send a gift of $500 which has continued monthly for several years. Whether we believe it or not, God knows our needs and our deadlines and is ready and willing to assist us on our journey of faith.

A Family's War Debt

According to scripture, personal and family debts are a continuing liability. It was 1968, I made a quick call home from Travis AFB in California before boarding the flight to Vietnam. My brother-in-law, George Stout, asked if I had a stopover in Manila, to pay a war debt for him. He had told me how the Melcompton family on Bascelian Island had saved him and two shipmates during the war by hiding them under their floor after the Japanese sank their PT boat. There was no time with all the research planned in Saigon, but I filed the idea in the back of my mind. When things went wrong in Saigon and I ended up in Bangkok and then to the Philippines, I remembered my family's war debt.

> 27. **Do not withhold good from those to whom it is due, when it is in your power to act. 28.** <u>Do not say to your neighbor, "Come back tomorrow and I'll give it to you"— when you already have it with you.</u> (Proverbs 3:27-28 NIV)

Seeking permission to travel about 600 miles south of Manila to Zamboanga City and then on to Bascelian Island, about 25 miles off the cost of Mindanao, the military said I must get permission from the Philippine government. They simply said, *"No, it was too dangerous, because of the Moro tribe's uprising on Mindanao."* The Moros were Muslim rebels and had never been conquered: not the Spanish, the English, the Dutch, the Japanese or the Americans. They were hostile to Christians and military personnel. Told that an American Military Chaplain would be in great danger going into that area with the present state of civil unrest among the Moros, I decided the war debt was important.

Explaining that I wanted to pay a family war debt, the government changed their mind. They required me to sign a waiver that they were not responsible for my safety and gave me about three hours of special briefing on how to conduct myself in the area. With all the papers signed, I put on civilian clothes and boarded an old Philippine plane. It was a rattle trap, or death trap, but we made it to Zamboanga City along with a few pigs and chickens. The airplane looked more like a rural bus loaded with a few people, but lots of animals.

The only way to reach Bascelian Island was travel by boat in the open sea about 25 miles to the Sulu Archipelago. Purchasing a ticket for a twelve-passenger boat, but there were only four aboard. I was told it would not leave until the boat was full. They wanted the American to buy the empty seats. With limited time, I bought the balance of the tickets, so we could depart. As we traveled the twenty-five miles of open sea, we passed a number of small outriggers. One had a small boy perched on a beam at the bow no larger than my hand. I commented to a passenger how dangerous it looked for a child to ride up there. I was told that the boy was spotting fish for his father and that if he were to fall the father would not even extend a paddle to him. He would have to swim and catch up on his own. When I appeared shocked at such paternal disdain, the man responded, *"He probably has four or five other sons at home; he would just bring another one on the next trip."* Finally, we arrived on the Island.

At the dock, I asked for directions to the home of Zoilo Melcompton. He was well known on the Island, and his home was easy to find. There were voices inside the house, so I knocked on the door. A middle-aged woman opened the door. I ask for Zoilo. A small man appeared and looked at me, surprised to see an American. When I said, "George Stout, sent me," the man screamed and slammed the door, and I heard him running up the stairs. Shocked, I slowly walked toward the steps assuming Zoilo didn't want anything to do with anyone who knew George. I was confused.

Hearing the door open, I turned to see Zoilo holding a large brown tube; I thought it was a bazooka. He saw the fear in my eyes and said, *"For George, I make for George a map of Philippines."* He unrolled the tube; it was a closely woven mat that included a map of the Philippine Islands with the words "George Stout" at the bottom.

George had corresponded with him for several years, but Zoilo's most recent Christmas card to George was returned marked, *"No forwarding address."* Zoilo assumed George would not write anymore. He had planned to ship the straw mat/map to George for Christmas but did not have a working address. I agreed to take it back to America. After expressing thanks for their efforts to save American Sailors, I paid what I could on the war debt. Perhaps it was the thought that counted with Zoilo. The risk of traveling from Manila to Bascelian through dangerous territory made my presence and the small gifts have value. Gifts cannot be measured by normal coinage value of the local economy, but by the cost to the giver. As a casualty of a war of nerves, I was ready to leave that dangerous place, but I was still thinking of the young men in harm's way on the battlefields of Vietnam.

> *7. **Pay what you owe: taxes to whom taxes are due; custom duties to whom payment is due;** look at and pay attention to those entitled to respect; honor to those entitled to honor. 8. **Leave no debt unpaid, except the debt of love to others:** for he who loves his neighbor has done what the law demands.* (Romans 13:7-8 EDNT)

> *1* A good name is more desirable than great riches; to be esteemed is better than silver or gold. *2* Rich and poor have this in common: The LORD is the Maker of them all. (Proverbs 22:1-2 NIV)

Jesus and Peter's Taxes

Peter was a fisherman but had no money for taxes. In a conversation with Jesus he was told to go fishing to get funds for the tax. Peter's first fish had a coin in its mouth that was "more than enough" so he was guided to pay both his and Jesus' taxes. The fish did not regurgitate the coinage on the shore as the Big Fish did with Jonah, Peter had to use his line and tackle and catch the fish. Where did the fish acquire the coin? Probably, some drunken fisherman dropped it overboard and the shining coin attracted the fish to take the bait. In this case someone else's loss was Peter's gain; *"the wealth of the sinner is stored for the hands of the righteous."* (Proverbs 13:22) This was not a miracle; it was simply kingdom economics at work. It was a blessing to Peter and taught a valuable lesson about paying taxes.

27. But lest we should cause them to stumble, go to the sea and cast a hook, and take up the first fish that comes up: and when you open its mouth, you will find a shekel: take that coin to the collectors for you and Me. (Matthew 17:27 EDNT)

Remain Focused

3. And I ask you also, true yokefellow, assist those women who labored with me in the gospel, with Clement also, and with others my fellow laborers, whose names are in the book of life. 4. Always rejoice in the Lord: and again, I say, rejoice. *5.* Let your gentleness be known to ever one. The Lord is at hand. *6. Be anxious for nothing; but under all circumstances by general prayer and specific petition joined with thanksgiving let your personal needs be known to God. 7. And the authentic peace of God which transcends all comprehension shall guard your hearts and minds through Christ Jesus. 8.* Finally, brethren, whatever things are genuine, whatever things are uncomplicated, whatever things are impartial, whatever things are unadulterated, whatever things are agreeable, whatever things are honorable; if there be any desirable quality, and if there be any acclaim, think on these things. *9. Model your behavior on those things which you both learned and received, and seen and heard of me, practice continually: and the God of peace will be with you.* (Philippians 4:3-9 EDNT)

1. Paul and Timothy, bondservants of Jesus Christ, to all the saints in Christ Jesus who are at Philippi, with the elders and ministers: 2. grace and peace to you from the Lord Jesus Christ. 3. Each occasion of my remembrance of you is a cause for thanksgiving, 4. always in my every prayer for you my request is with joy, 5. on account of your partnership in the gospel until this moment; 6. being persuaded that He who began a good work in you will carry it out until the day of Jesus Christ: 7. I have you in my heart and it is right for me to think this of you; inasmuch as both in my bonds, and in the defense and confirmation of the gospel, you are partakers of my grace. (Philippians 1:1-7 EDNT)

*15. You Philippians know that in the beginning of the gospel, when I departed for Macedonia, no assembly but you, **shared with me concerning financial matters.** 16. For even in Thessalonica you sent funds twice to provide for my needs. 17. It was not a desire for financial gifts: but I desired that a harvest may abound to your account. 18. But I have more than enough: my needs are fully satisfied, having received of Epaphroditus the gifts you sent, they were like a sweet-smelling sacrifice acceptable and well pleasing to God. 19. But **my God shall supply all your needs according to the wealth of His glory by Christ Jesus.** 20. Now to God our Father be praises for ever and ever. Amen. (Philippians 4:15-20 EDNT)*

XII

Managing Business, Health and Spirituality

Water of Life is Free

God is the source of all prosperity and blessings in the lives of mankind. Where the heart is there will be treasures that flow in love and blessings to others. When the spirit of Christ is in the heart it is like a spring in the desert, flowing to refresh all who travel near the oasis of faith. The water of life is free to all and should be shared freely. In fact, the Jesus was clear, *"Whosoever gives even a cup of cold water because he is a disciple shall be rewarded."* Matthew 10:32 EDNT) It is the author's assumption that spirituality is central to both personal business and physical health. Morality that leads to ethical living and positive dealings with others creates good will for business and enhances the personal lives of those involved in the social transactions.

> *14. but <u>whoever drinks of the water that I give shall never thirst;</u> **but the water that I shall give him shall be in him a well of water springing up to everlasting life.** (John 4:14 EDNT) 6. I am Alpha and Omega, the beginning and the end. **I will give to him***

who is athirst of the fountain of the water of life without price. (Revelation 21:6 EDNT)

Spirituality is Apparent in Business Matters

Doing business in Bible days was totally different from the incorporated climate of today. There were no charters, business licenses, payroll taxes, etc., it was a simple a personal interaction to buy, sell, or barter with a neighbor, friend, or traveler to generate goods and services in support of family and others. Business matters were occupational. In reality all business was dealings with others in a manner that netted something of value. Honest achievement in transacting "business" was tied to faith and integrity and for believers it was closely related to true spiritual lifestyle and reliability.

Walking in Truth and Faithfulness

John (3 John 1:2-8) desired, Gaius, a personal friend, achievement in business affairs and that he would remain safe and ambulatory in physical health. However, John was not promising prosperity or physical health, only desiring this for his friend. Why not promise, because John saw prosperity and health as being related to the quality of a spiritual lifestyle; true prosperity was somehow connected to the essence of soul care and spiritual commitment. John was writing about the soul in a spiritual sense because Gaius was definitely *"walking in truth and faithfulness"* in contrast to Diotrephes who ridiculed the gospel messengers and rejected the message of truth. With a malicious tongue, Diotrephes had rejected the brethren with whom he disagreed and banished them from the daily gathering of believers. Diotrephes was not showing the necessary ethical commitment to spiritually prosper.

> *2. Beloved, concerning all things I pray that you may* **prosper in business and be safe and sound in body, as your soul prospers.** *3. For I rejoiced greatly when some brothers came bearing witness of you in truth,* **as you in truth walk.** *4. I have no greater joy than to hear that my children are walking in truth. 5. Beloved you are faithfully serving when you show kindness to the brethren, even when they are strangers to you. 6. And they testify of your love before the assembly: if you send them on their journey as godly men, you do well: 7. because they went out for His name's sake, taking nothing from the Gentiles. 8.* **It is a duty to support such men, that we may show ourselves fellow workers with the truth.** (3 John 1:2-8 EDNT)

An Old Testament Record of Business

The Jewish people did not allow buying and selling on the Sabbath, but when secular merchants and sellers of all kinds of ware lodged without the gates of Jerusalem ready for business on the Sabbath, they were warned not to return. (Nehemiah 13:20-21) Another example is that of a widow who came to Elisha about a creditor pressing for her husband's debt. Elisha asked what she had in her house. The answer was a pot of oil. As she followed the guidance of the Prophet, miraculously the pot filled many barrowed pots and she complied with his advice: *Go, sell the oil, and pay the debt, and you and the children live on the rest. (Read 2 Kings 4:1-7)*

Matthew's Record of Buying and Selling

In Matthew's gospel, the story of how the kingdom of heaven was similar to young women taking their lamps to meet the bridegroom. Half foolishly took lamps with no oil and asked others to share. They were told *"go to those who sell and by for yourselves, lest there not be enough for all of us."* (Matthew 2:7 -9) This illustrates those who were unprepared and others who would not share. Elsewhere Matthew compares the kingdom of heaven with individual greed in the buying and selling of a merchant who wanted a costly pearl and sold all he had in order to purchase the one rare jewel for himself. (Matthew 13:45-46) Such careless and greedy dealings of putting "all the eggs in one basket" could hinder the advancement of the kingdom of God. There is no place in the band of believers for greed, stinginess or those who withhold funds from the needy.

Luke's Report in Acts

Luke shared in Acts 2 how early believers considering their personal possessions as common property to be sold and distributed to the needs of others. By agreement, they met daily to break bread from house to house and took meals cheerfully. This commitment bought believers favor with the community and the Lord added to their number daily those being saved. (Acts 2:44-47) However, this short-lived system did not last because of the selfishness and greed of some.

A Lack of Spirituality Caused a Downfall

An agreed transaction to sell land to raise funds for the common need of the Apostles went badly because one couple kept back part of the price and lied about the amount of the sale. (Acts 5:8) This was a volunteer system and they had the right to keep some of the proceeds of the land sale for their personal needs. The problem was the intentional falsehood about the sale price of the property. This brought a sense of "personal and spiritual discipline" to the faith-promise system of raising funds. Both the couple and the congregation greatly suffered loss because of their lack of truthfulness. The lack of honesty and true spirituality certainly had a role in their status and ultimate downfall.

A Devout Business Woman

In Acts 16:13-15 Luke reports on Paul's travels where he came to Philippi and participated in a Sabbath prayer service for women by the river. A devout business woman, Lydia, seller of purple cloth, attended prayer service and the Lord opened her heart as she listened to the words of Paul. Afterwards she and her household were baptized, and she appealed to the ministry team to lodge at her house. This demonstrates that sincere worship and business were logically joined, and the Cause of Christ and Christianity was advanced.

On another occasion, Paul recommended Phoebe to the church in Rome and asked that they assist her business, because she was a believer and was helpful to others.

> *1. I commend to you Phoebe our sister, who is a leader in the congregation at Cenchrea: 2.* **welcome her in the Lord as a believer and provide any assistance she may need in her business: for she has been most helpful in a difficult situation for many including myself.** *3. Remember me to Priscilla and Aquila my fellow-workers in Christ Jesus: 4. who risked their own lives to save my life: unto whom not only I give thanks, but all the congregations of the Gentiles. 5. Also, give greetings to the congregation that meets in their house.* (Romans 16:1-16 EDNT)

Paul's use of "prosper"

Paul used the same word for "prosper" in Romans and Corinthians when he wrote about a safe and healthful journey and identified their gifts as being related to and resulting from being spiritually prosperous.

> *8. First, I continue to thank my God through Jesus Christ for all of you, because your faith is proclaimed all over the world. 9. Calling God to witness, whom I serve with my spirit in the gospel of His Son, how spontaneously I always include you in my prayers; 10. Making requests* **that my whole journey to you would be prosperous by the will of God.** *11. I have a yearning to see you and* **impart some spiritual endowment to establish you in the faith;** *12. that I may be encouraged together with you by our mutual faith. (Romans 1:8-12 EDNT)*

> *1 Now concerning the gathering of funds for the saints, follow the directions I gave to the congregations of Galatia. 2. On the first day of*

each week **remember how God has prospered you and put aside your gifts in a safe place,** *so no collections will be necessary when I come. (1* Corinthians 16:1-2 EDNT)

A Recognizable Lifestyle Characteristic

The record in Acts makes clear that systematic teaching and learning in the process of "making disciples" creates a trait in believers that is identifiable and recognizable by local folk outside the assembly. *And for one whole year they assembled with the congregation and taught many people. And the disciples (learners) first began* **to transact their affairs (business) as Messiah-like people in Antioch.** (Acts 11: 26 EDNT) This behavior was observed by the secular businessmen of Antioch. At first being a Christian disciple was a lifestyle and was recognized by others; then it became a mark of identification as a follower of Jesus Christ. Those who walked in fellowship with Jesus and others were expected to develop a missional lifestyle and work to support their family and kingdom endeavors. Jesus made it clear at an early age (Luke 2:40 EDNT) that He must be involved in spiritual matters because He felt compelled to be about "**His Father's Business.**"

Love is the Issue

Paul was concerned about the fruit of the Spirit which was love working in the lives of believers. *But set your hearts on the best spiritual graces: and yet I can show you a way beyond all comparison.* (1 Corinthians 12:31 EDNT) That way was "love" and this acrostic clearly explains the word:

L-earning from the past;

O-pening your heart to others;

V-iewing the future with faith, and

E-njoying the present moment.

13. Brethren, God called you to freedom; but do not make your freedom an excuse for a corrupt nature, but by love serve one another. 14. For the whole law is fulfilled in one word, even love; you shall love your neighbor as yourself. 15. But if you bite and devour one another, take heed lest you are destroyed by one another. 16. This I say, **continue to walk in the Spirit, and you will not at all satisfy the desires of the flesh.** *17. The flesh and the Spirit are opposing each other: the flesh combats the Spirit, and the Spirit combats the flesh: this is why you cannot do all the things you would do. 18. But if you are guided by the Spirit, you no longer need to follow the law. 19.* **Now the behavior that belongs to the flesh is obvious, they are: (sensual sins) unfaithfulness in marriage, unrestrained living, unbridled acts of indecency; 20. (religious sins) the worship of idols, the use of drugs and magical powers; (temperamental sins) hostility, strife, jealousy, violent flare-ups of temper, self-seeking ambitions, adherence to contradictory teaching; 21.(personal sins) desires to appropriate what others have, drunkenness and carousing, and similar things:** *I warned you before that people who do such things will have no part in the kingdom of God. 22.* **But the fruit of the Spirit is love, and love brings joy, peace, longsuffering, gentleness, goodness, faith, 23. tolerance and self-control: and no law exists against any of these.** *24. And those who belong to Christ have nailed the flesh to the cross with its* *passions and appetites. 25. Since we live in the Spirit, we should be guided by the Spirit in our orderly walk. 26. Let us not have excessive pride or boastfulness about personal abilities, infuriating one another or causing others to be enviou*s. (Galatians 5:13-26 EDNT)

The Love of Money

Paul was troubled about how the materialistic world could influence converts to Christianity. He warned young Timothy about the love of money and told him to be on guard against greed. Paul told the congregation at Corinth about association with sexual immorality and included *"put away from among yourselves the greedy man."* It appears that immorality and greed can corrupt others and hinder their spiritual growth. physical health, and personal productivity.

7. For we brought nothing into this world, neither can we carry out anything. 8. Let us be content with food and clothing. 9. **But those who are determined to be rich are tempted and caught in a trap, and into many senseless and dangerous appetites,** *such desires cause men to sink into present destruction and later punishment in hell.* 10. **For the root of all evil is the love of money: while some craving money have wandered away from the faith and suffered many self-inflicted and discouraging sorrows.** (1 Timothy 6:7-10 EDNT)

11. But now I have written to you **not to associate intimately with any man so called a brother who is sexually immoral**, *a covetous man, an idolater, or one who speaks reproachfully or a drunkard or* **a greedy man**, *with such do not even eat. 12. For is it* *my business to judge those outside the assembly? Is it yours to judge those within the assembly? 13. But the outsiders God will judge,* **therefore, you put away from among yourselves that wicked person.** *(1 Corinthians 5:10-13 EDNT)*

Be on Guard against Greed

Scripture is clear that the life of a believer should not be based on personal prosperity. ***Be on guard against greed: for a man's life is not based on wealth or possessions.*** *(Luke 12:15 EDNT)* This is a controlling factor in a missional lifestyle. Consideration must be given to the needs of others and the advancement of the kingdom. To concentrate on the accumulation of material things while neglecting the concerns of others, is a gross violation of true religion and the spirit of evangelism. Surely, one must be aware of the spiritual issues of life including the business of making a living by honest and healthy means and the overriding issues of spiritual commitments to family, the children's inheritance, the proper and scriptural used of resources and true devotion to spiritual matters.

Spirituality is Obvious in Health Issues

The scriptural reward of unrighteousness is self-destruction. The unredeemed follow their natural instincts to do evil and the result is a troubled life filled with sickness caused by Prodigal Son behavior of extravagance and waste. When divine blessings provide resources for family support, the children's inheritance, and an overage for the poor and kingdom advance are misused, there is no hopeful future for such individuals. Scripture is clear: the wealth of those who miss the mark and gain riches deceitfully will eventually become losers: *Dishonest wealth will become steadily less,* **but those who gather by labor will have an increase in assets.** (Proverb 13:11 EDOT)

An Honored Seat at the Table

17. A corrupt go-between stumbles into sorrow: but **a trustworthy mentor ensures health.** *18. Poverty and disgrace follow those who refuse instruction:* **but he who respects a warning shall have an honored seat at the table.** (Proverbs 13:17-18 EDOT)

Conditional Health

And the Lord laid before them these conditions, "If you listen carefully to the LORD your God and do what is right in his eyes, if you pay attention to his commands and keep them, **I will not bring on you any of the diseases I brought on the Egyptians, for I am the LORD, who heals you.**" (Exodus 15:25 EDOT)

Never too Big to Fail

Ephesus was the chief city Asia and one of the most important business and cultural centers in the Roman Empire. Ephesus had a prominent Christian congregation in the area served by Paul, Peter, and John, with John being the leader at the time of his exile to Patmos. Although in John's time it was on the coast, it is now several miles inland due to natural changes in the coastline. Paul spent a great deal of time at Ephesus and other churches established in his missionary travel and expressed concern by

letter that some had left their first love. They had
steadfast endurance and had labored in God's
name, but they did not habitually behave in love.
The ruins of Ephesus have been extensively
excavated. However, the Candlestick of the
Ephesian Congregation was jeopardized by
this lack of love. This was a problem **then** and
remains a problem **now** in congregations which
do not manifest the fruit of the Spirit – *love* -- and
all the byproducts of divine love to each other and
the lost world.

Paul's Warning

Paul warned a great church about *"callous
greediness"* and "*reckless spendthrift*" in the list of
people with whom believers should never associate.
(vs.3-5) Why, because greedy, wasteful, extravagant,
and irresponsible people are bad news for kingdom
economics and personal wealth designed to support
families, their legacy, faith-based entities, and
missional outreach to the lost and needy.

> *1. Become imitators of God, as His beloved children;*
> *2. and **habitually behave in love**, as Christ loved*
> *you, and was delivered for you as an offering and*
> *voluntary sacrifice to God to become a pleasing*
> *fragrance. 3. But as saints let not immorality,*
> impurity or ***callous greediness, be named even***
> *once among you; 4. neither obscenity, nor corrupt*
> *talking, nor practiced suggestive speech, these are all*
> *unbecoming behavior: but rather give thanks. 5. For*
> *this you surely know, that no solicitor for prostitutes,*
> *or **reckless spendthrift**, or worshiper of idols, will*
> *have a place in the kingdom of Christ and of God. 6.*

Let no man mislead you with words devoid of truth: because these things bring the anger of God upon the disobedient. 7. **Do not associate with such things. 8. For once your heart was in darkness, but now it is filled with light from the Lord: behave as the product of light: 9. (for the product of light is seen in all goodness, righteousness, and sincerity; 10. be living proof of what is well-pleasing to the Lord.** 11. And have no friendship with the activities of darkness, but rather admonish them. *(*Ephesians 5:1-11 EDNT)

Peter Wrote about Spirituality

The hotheaded sailor, Peter, had some soft words about the believer's spiritual calling, lifestyle and prosperity. His goal was for believers to maintain the enduring characteristics of agreeableness, benevolence, compassion, devotion, and faithfulness. Peter was quoting from Psalm 34:12-15 about "good days" from the divine perspective. A "good day" for a believer comes with Divine assistance and blessings in spite of human difficulties. A good day is to prosper in business affairs, walk in health, receive answers to prayers, *and experience the goodness and nearness of God, then a believer can say:*

This is the day the Lord has made, I will rejoice and be glad in it!

(Psalm 118:24)

The incentives to spend, borrow, and take unnecessary risk in an effort to get rich, cripples many who are unprepared for the real world of economics and personal wealth.

About The Author

Hollis L. Green, ThD, PhD, DLitt, is a Clergy-Educator with public relations and business credentials and doctorates in theology, education, and  philosophy. A Distinguished Professor of Education and Social Change at the graduate level for over three decades, Dr. Green is a Diplomate in the Oxford Society of Scholars, and author of 50+ books and numerous articles. He served six years as a member of the U.S. Senate Business Advisory Board and with certified membership in several public relations societies (RPRC, PRSA, and IPRC). He served pastorates in five states, was a denominational official for 18 years, and traveled in ministry and lectured in over 100 countries.

Dr. Green was the founder (1974) of Associated Institutional Developers (AID) Ltd., an international Public Relations and Corporate Consultant Company. He was Vice-President (1974-1979) of Luther Rice Seminary (www.lru.edu) and became the founding President (1981) and Chancellor (1991-2008) of Oxford Graduate School, [www.ogs.edu]. As part of a global outreach, Dr. Green founded OASIS UNIVERSITY (2002) in Trinidad, W. I. [www.oasisedu.org] where he continues to lecture and teach and assist the administration as Chancellor. In 2004, he assisted in establishing Greenleaf Global Educational Foundation in Colorado to advance issues related to the current needs of society.

In addition to his other endeavors, Dr. Green launched Global Educational Advance, Inc. (2007) [www.gea-books.com] to advance higher education and social change through publishing, curriculum development, library/ learning resources, instruction, and global book distribution with 30,000 distributors in 100 countries to advance social change. His books and assisting authors in publishing are a logical outgrowth of a sixty-year ministry through education. He serves the Author/Publisher Partnership PRESS as Corporate Chair and Co-publisher with his sons, Barton and Brian. Dr. Green continues to travel, speak, teach, write books and work with authors in publishing.

Appendix –A

Operational Definitions

- **Credit--** *the means to live beyond your income.*

- **Debt –** *encumbering the future for present convenience*

- **Donation --** *a gift is <u>shared overage</u> from having "more than enough."*

- **Economics --** *related to the management of income, expenses, money or wealth.*

- **Gifts--** *are valued in terms of the cost to the giver.*

- **Green and Brown Money--** *green money is recently earned and contains sweat equity while brown money is savings, gifts, or unearned income. The older the money the browner it gets. Green money is part of personal wealth; brown money is "more than enough" for family needs and is designed to support kingdom work.*

- **Kingdom economics --** *the careful management of available providential (care and guidance of God) resources or the thriftiness of careful budgeting.*

- ***Missional Lifestyle**--understanding the thinking, behaving, and practices of a missionary.*

- ***Personal wealth**—the funds one personally manages for the good of the Kingdom.*

- ***Poverty or Scarcity**-- the fundamental economic problem of having unlimited needs and wants in a world of limited resources.*

- ***Sacrificial Gift** – giving beyond one's normal ability influenced by a spiritual desire.*

- ***Secular Economics**-- knowledge concerned with the production, consumption, and transfer of wealth: in short **"material prosperity."***

- ***Spiritual Equity**—is the coinage value added to a gift because of what it cost the giver.*

- ***Stewardship**—responsibility for arranging financial issues for the benefit of family, others, and/or kingdom issues.*

- ***Sweat Equity**—is the "value added" over and above the monetary significance of a personal gift or kingdom investment based on the physical energy expended by the donor beyond the coinage value of the donation.*

- ***Wealth** -- literally wages enough for a living and a plentiful supply of essential things with "more than enough" to share with others.*

Appendix B

Accounting for Volunteer Labor

What is the monetary value of volunteer time?

The estimated value of volunteer time for 2016 was $24.14 per hour, according to Independent Sector, a coalition of charities, foundations, corporations, and individuals that publishes research important to the nonprofit sector. It reports annual statistics on the estimated dollar value of volunteer time, including historical values back to 1980 and values for each state. (Note, there is a lag of almost one year in the government's release of data.)

More statistics on volunteers in the US and abroad can be found on Energize, Inc.'s-- Statistics on Volunteering page.

Nonprofits typically use the value of volunteer time to demonstrate the support they receive from their communities. Independent Sector advises that if your organization plans to report the value of volunteer services in external financial statements, including grant proposals, you will need to follow generally accepted accounting principles (GAAP), established by the Financial Accounting Standards Board (FASB), which state:

- Contributions of services shall be recognized if the services received: create or enhance nonfinancial assets; or require specialized skills, are provided by individuals possessing those skills, and would typically need to be purchased if not provided by donation. Services requiring specialized skills are provided by accountants, architects, carpenters, doctors, electricians, lawyers, nurses, plumbers, teachers, and other professionals and craftsmen.

- <u>Per IRS</u>, nonprofits may not report volunteer time as contributions in line 1 of Parts II or III of Form 990, Schedule A. **It may be described in Form 990, Part III, *Statement of Program Service Accomplishments***

Volunteers may be the only human
beings who truly reflect the compassion,
unselfish caring, patience, and love
for others, that we all should possess.
Volunteers do not just have the time; they
have the heart to do for others. One lives by
what they earn; they make a life by what
they share.

Appendix C

THE LEARNING CENTRE

Available options with qualified teachers, certificates
of completion and participation honors

OPTIONS:

(1)

The Academy (K-12) + options
K-3; K-6; K-9; K-12; or APT

Academic Performance Training of Students

"Helping Every-age Learn Proficiently"

(2)

C.A.F.E.©
COMMUNITY AND FAMILY EDUCATION©

**Providing Practical Bible Study, Lifestyle Training for
Family Life, Community Service, and
Faith-based Personal Ministry.**

(3)

(4)

Yeshiva Torah Institute

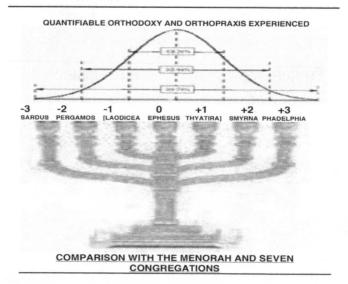

COMPARISON WITH THE MENORAH AND SEVEN CONGREGATIONS

Climbing the ladder toward New Testament Judaism

(5)

Church and Faith-based subjects presented in Workshops, Seminars, and Specialized Classes for Serious Learners, PLUS Academic Performance Training (academic guidance for High School and College Students).

Train the young in the ways of the Lord
and when they are old they will remember.

APPENDIX D

Y.E.S. FUNDING

Yearly Endowed Support

THE LEARNING CENTRE is a not-for-profit venture to extend the Faith-based services of New Life Baptist Church to the community and the needs of Faith-based families and groups in the area, and as such depends on donations from supporters. While businesses rely on sales and governments depend on taxes/appropriations, a nonprofit enterprise is sustained in large part by voluntary contributions. Although THE LEARNING CENTRE AT NEW LIFE receives fees for textbooks, syllabi material, etc., such sources are never enough to operate effective learning programs for biblical, community, and family-based study.

THE LEARNING CENTRE is a moral and intellectual effort, equipping believers to become problem-solvers and effective servant leaders to advance the cause of Christ. It is a specialized Faith-based program primarily sponsored by members and friends of New Life Baptist Church. The cost of operation is not charged to students. Friends assist in underwriting the annual operating budget. Donors may assist the operation of THE LEARNING CENTRE by regular donations, just as many do with missional gifts for their place of worship. The Y.E.S. Fund is supported by the generosity of Friends.

Y. E. S. FUNDING

A number of individuals and families share in the **Y**early **E**ndowed **S**ecurity Budget by assisting in the support of the expenses involved in C.A.F.E./A.I.M. studies. THE LEARNING CENTRE invites individuals, businesses, organizations, and families to consider giving to assist Faith-based learning through the Y.E.S. Project that supports the various aspects of the Community and Family programs for the Tri-Cities area. Will you say "YES" to participation and support?

INDIVIDUAL SUPPORT

As an interested individual, I wish to contribute to THE LEARNING CENTRE Y.E.S. Fund to support the specialized learning opportunities for worthy and serious learners. [ ] Here is my Annual gift of _____;
[ ] my monthly gift of _____; or
[ ] my one-time gift of _____ to support this work.

Name_____

Address _____

Telephone _____ Email _____

Signed: _____Date_____

Contact: THE LEARNING CENTRE

PO Box 335, 100 Hendrickson Lane, Bluff City, TN 37618, 423-338-9017

AREA CHURCH SPONSORSHIP

THE LEARNING CENTRE would appreciate an opportunity to partner with area local churches and Faith-based groups in training promising young men and women for leadership, community service, and practical ministry roles in the church and community. The Y.E.S. Fund is an excellent opportunity to provide training assistance for young men and women who will become the next level of Faith-based leadership in the community and families of the area. Area Churches are encouraged to sponsor promising local leadership as participants from their congregation who share in the advanced learning opportunities provided. **THE LEARNING CENTRE, PO Box 335, 100 Hendrickson Lane, Bluff City, TN 37618, 423-338-9017**

BUSINESS AND CORPORATE SPONSORSHIP

Corporate and business operations with a sense of social and community responsibility may contribute to THE LEARNING CENTRE through Y.E.S. Funding or sponsor specific young men and women for these specialized learning opportunities offered by C.A.F.E. or A.I.M. This is a good long-term investment for family and community. **Contact THE LEARNING CENTRE, PO Box 335, 100 Hendrickson Lane, Bluff City, TN 37618, 423-338-9017,**

Global Educational Advance, Inc.

Email: greenoxon2@gmail.com for a 75-pp PDF "A 2018 COLLECTIVE REPORT" covering this Global ministry through education for the past 45 years. (See): www.gea-books.com or www.globalaim.net for more data.

APPENDIX E

FAMILY BUDGET ASSISTANCE

(This author is pleased to recommend Dave Ramsey's Plan)

A family budget will help you know where your money is going and stop want you wondering where it went. Dave Ramsey has a Christian perspective on budgeting and wealth. For assistance go to: ***https://www. everydollar.com/app/sign-up/daveramsey***

Budgeting Just Got Easy

Budget from your computer, iPhone or Android device with Every Dollar, Dave's **FREE** budget tool that is helping people knock out debt, build wealth, and start living!

Budget on the Go

Create a budget, manage money, and track spending on the go with the EveryDollar budget apps for iPhone and Android. EveryDollar syncs across devices, so whether you are budgeting from your desktop or phone, your budget is always up to date.

- **Easy Budgeting** No more pen, paper or complicated spreadsheets
- **Helpful Visuals** Quick views for what's planned, spent and remaining

- **Secure Data** Access EveryDollar across devices with bank-level security
- **Proven Plan** Based on Dave's Baby Steps to beat debt and build wealth
- **Create Your Account Button** You agree to EveryDollar's Terms of Use.
- **Budget Your Way with EveryDollar** With both free and premium plans available, you can budget how you choose!

All EveryDollar budgeters receive a free trial of EveryDollar Plus.

✓ Create unlimited budgets

✓ Track transactions against your budget

✓ Email Support

✓ Connect to your bank for faster expense tracking

✓ View account balances within EveryDollar

Call-back support and coaching calls

Common Sense Economics
Key Elements of Practical Personal Finance

Some say single-minded pursuit of money and wealth is the key to happiness.

A Student Practice Questionnaire

1. Your comparative advantage in a specific area is determined by

Answer: the market value of the skill relative to your opportunity cost of supplying it.

2. Financial insecurity in America is primarily the result of

Answer: a low rate of personal saving and poor financial planning and a shortage of financial planners and portfolio managers.

3. Economic analysis indicates

Answer: no matter what our objectives in life, they are easier to achieve if we have more wealth.

4. Compared to graduates, high school drop outs are

Answer: more likely to be poor.

5. Which of the following is true?

Answer: If you want to make a lot of money, you had better figure out how to provide others with substantial value and find ways to discover and act on valuable opportunities.

6. Which of the following is the best example of an item that a "real world" savings account is designed to cover?

Answer: an unexpected expenditure to repair the transmission of your car.

7. Deferred tax saving plans such as a Roth Individual Retirement Account (IRA) or 401k plan will

Answer: reduce your current tax liability because funds paid into these plans are tax deductible.

8. Which of the following is an advantage of an indexed equity mutual fund relative to a managed equity fund? Answer: Indexed funds have lower operating costs because they engage in less stock trading.

9. The random walk theory indicates that

Answer: changes in stock prices are driven by surprise occurrences that are difficult to predict.

10. The variation in the rate of return one can expect from ownership of stocks will generally be smaller

Answer: if a diverse set of stocks is held over a lengthy period of time such as 30 or 40 years.

11. Buying shares of corporate stock tends to be risky when

Answer: all of the above are true.

12. If an investor's primary stock holding is currently Exxon Mobil, the purchase of which of the following stocks would provide the investor with the largest reduction in risk?

Answer: Wal-Mart.

13. Which of the following has enhanced the ability of investors, without any special business skills, to benefit from the ownership of corporate America?

a. the increased availability of mutual funds, that make it possible for even small investors to purchase a diverse stock portfolio at a low cost

b. an increased tendency of small investors to buy and sell stock frequently

c. the virtual disappearance of business failures among corporations with publicly traded stock shares

d. all of the above

14. Which of the following is true?

Answer: An investment strategy that yielded a high rate of return in the past will often be disastrous in the future.

15. Which of the following is the best analogy to describe the power of compound interest?

Answer: a snowball rolling down a snow-covered mountain, growing in size as it descends d. a penny dropped from the top of a very tall building, gathering speed as it falls

16. Which of the following is a risk associated with investing in bonds?

Answer: All of the above are risks associated with bond investments.

17. It is often substantially cheaper to own and operate a used car rather than a new one because

Answer: the depreciation cost for a new car will almost always be substantially higher.

18. Which of the following items would be most dangerous to purchase on credit

Answer: a vacation and a college education

19. Which of the following financial strategies will help you increase your wealth and future level of income?

Answer: All of the above will help you build wealth.

20. Many Americans feel financially insecure primarily because

Answer: the personal saving rate of Americans is low, and many spend more than they earn.

APPENDIX F

BASIC MONEY MANAGEMENT SKILLS

Planning for the future is essential. Learning about financial Planning, banking, investment advisers, and protecting money and assets is vital to young people. Caregivers should focus on guiding youth aged 9-17 years to think beyond their direct circumstances and adopt the values that will enable them to establish a more viable economic future for themselves. This will assure a sense of self-worth, personal and community responsibility, integrity and a 1sense of industry. This age group must be exposed to an appreciation for and the value of money and its uses. They also need information about the principles and practices of business and economy.

When a child treats money as if it grows on trees or magically falls from the sky, caregivers and guardians must teach them the true meaning of money. The primary lesson that must be learned relates to the exchange of energy for money, and money for energy. If one has money, they may hire someone to do the work. If one has energy, they may obtain work to acquire money. Perhaps each child could learn from this exchange between father and son:

"No mon-- no fun, your son!"

"Too bad-- so sad, your dad!"

Regardless of age with a little assistance children can develop the self-confidence and personal skills needed to adequately manage money. Everyone has to deal with 174 Remedial and Surrogate Parenting both energy and money. Research shows that people worry more about money than any other family or personal problem. Here are four basic concepts in the adequate handling of money.

1. Developing self-control in spending is a basic step in cutting the cost of living. Some individuals instinctively know how to get what they want, even on a limited income. Others need more guidance in managing finances to get what they need and want.

2. If everyone understands the financial situation, there will be greater cooperation. A spending plan or budget to allocate income to cover expenses is a necessary step. This is a simple concept, but a challenging task for many.

3. Everyone must learn to live within their means (earnings) rather that adapting the false notion that good credit gives them the means to live beyond their income. As my grandfather said, **When your outgo is more than your income, your upkeep will be your downfall.**

4. Learning to save part of one's income is the key to having enough later. This is a plan not just for a "rainy day;" it is required to avoid financial disaster. Teaching basic money

management skills to young children through savings accounts is a great way to prepare children for the real world and the reality of debt.

Show children the value of money by encouraging them to save money from allowance or odd jobs. When it is "their money," they learn the lessons quickly. Here are some thoughts about "money matters" that were passed to my sons:

Money is about the future! Each and every financial transaction must be weighed with reference to expectations of forthcoming expenses. A purchase is not about the present; it always relates to the future. Is this purchase absolutely necessary? Do I have sufficient funds to make this purchase? Does it use funds that will be required for future obligations? Do I have pressing future obligations that this purchase makes impossible?

Consequently, everyone must have a contingency plan relative to money. In the case of a Bank Account, an overdraw privilege is for an emergency not a regular occurrence. It is expensive to use the banks money. For example, a $36. overdraft is 10% interest on $360 or 20% interest on $720. Such expenses rob your future. A limited "safety net" is the best solution. Establish a savings account of $200 in your name and tie it to the account for overdraft protection. The balance in such an account should always be at least $200. The goal for such a savings is to have sufficient Funds to operate one month without expected income. One cannot spend anticipated funds or live on credit. This always complicates the future.

Technically, everyone has a short fall, unexpected expenses, and emergencies. Advance planning is necessary to avert damage and loss. It would be good if you anticipated what one month of expenses could be. Consider these 10 things.

1. Mortgage or rent
2. Food and medicine
3. Utilities
4. Car expenses including anticipated trips
5. Insurance and taxes
6. Entertainment
7. Required savings
8. All income must be divided into expense and savings.
9. When funds are received deposit some in checking and some in savings.
10. Avoid any behavior or action that could cause unexpected expenses: such as, traffic tickets, overdrafts, breakage of equipment or loss or neglect of property.

All caregivers need the brochure: *"A Parent's Guide to Youth Money Management,"* presented by the Manitoba Securities Commission: www.mbsecurities.ca/get-informed/pubs/mic_guide.pdf

Another guide called *Make it Count: An Instructor's Guide to Youth Money Management* is designed in parallel to the Parent's guide by topic but differs in format. It has actual lesson plans and black line masters for instructors to use with the outlined activities. A copy of the guide may be viewed on the web site:

www.makeitcountonline.ca.

Youth Money Management (FREE download)

There are many other things that Jesus
said and did, and if they were all written,
even the world itself could not hold the
books.

(John 21:25)

Bibliography

General Economics

Alan L. Gustman, Thomas L. Steinmeier and Nahid Tabatabai (2012) 'Financial Knowledge and Financial Literacy at the Household Level', *The American Economic Review*. American Economic Association American Economic Association, 102(3), pp. 309–313. Available at: http://www.jstor.org/stable/23245548?pq-origsite=summon&seq=1#page_scan_tab_contents.

Ashurst, L. (2009) *Talking About Retirement: The Secrets of Successful Retirement Planning*. 1st edn. London: Kogan Page. Available at: http://northumbria.eblib.com/patron/FullRecord.aspx?p=433147.

Baker, H. K. and Ricciardi, V. (2014) *Investor Behavior: The Psychology of Financial Planning and Investing*. 1st edn. Hoboken: Wiley. Available at: http://northumbria.eblib.com/patron/FullRecord.aspx?p=1629166.

Bernstein, W. J. (2010a) *The Four Pillars of Investing: Lessons for Building a Winning Portfolio*. Available at: https://www.dawsonera.com/guard/protected/dawson.jsp?name=https://login.northumbria.ac.uk/idp/shibboleth&dest=http://www.dawsonera.com/depp/reader/protected/external/AbstractView/S9780071759175.

Bernstein, W. J. (2010b) *The four pillars of investing: lessons for building a winning portfolio*. New York: McGraw-Hill.

Bodie, Z., Kane, A., Marcus, A. J. and Bodie, Z. (2011) *Investments and portfolio management*. 9th ed., [Global ed.]. New York: McGraw-Hill Irwin.

Cheung, C Sherman, Miu,Peter (no date) 'Home ownership decision in personal finance: some empirical evidence', *Financial Services Review*, 24(1), pp. 51–76. Available at: http://search.proquest.com/docview/1680949398?pq-origsite=summon&accountid=12860.

Dix, R. (2016) *Property investment for beginners*. Expanded and updated ed.

Dworsky, L. N. (2009a) *Understanding the Mathematics of Personal Finance: An Introduction to Financial Literacy*. 1st edn. Hoboken:

Wiley. Available at: http://northumbria.eblib.com/patron/
FullRecord.aspx?p=469363.

Fidelity International - ISAs, SIPPs, Funds Trusts (no date). Available at:
https://www.fidelity.co.uk/investor/default.page.

Fisher, A. (2010) *The Financial Times guide to inheritance tax, probate
and estate planning.* Harlow: Financial Times Prentice Hall.

*Free and impartial money advice, set up by government - Money Advice
Service* (no date). Available at: https://www.moneyadviceservice.
org.uk/en.

Genders, D. B. (2016) *The Daily Telegraph tax guide 2016: understanding
the tax system, completing your tax return and planning how to
become more tax efficient.* London: Kogan Page.

Gorham, J. (2008) *Mastering personal finance.* Basingstoke: Palgrave
Macmillan.

Greenwood, J. (2012) *The Financial times guide to pensions and wealth
in retirement.* 2nd ed. Harlow, England: Financial Times/Prentice
Hall.

Innovate Media (2015) *Insurance Basics: The Beginner Guide to Planning
Your Insurance.* CreateSpace.

Lawrenson, D. (2015) *Successful property letting: how to make money in
buy-to-let.* Expanded new edition. London: Robinson.

McCarthy, P. and Hatcher, C. (2010) *Presentation skills: the essential
guide for students.* Los Angeles: Sage. Available at: https://www.
dawsonera.com/guard/protected/dawson.jsp?name=https://
login.northumbria.ac.uk/idp/shibboleth&dest=http://www.
dawsonera.com/depp/reader/protected/external/AbstractView/
S9781446275801.

Melville, A. (2017a.b) *Taxation: Finance Act 2016.* Twenty-second
edition. Harlow, England: Pearson.

Mitchell, P. of C. L. and C. J. B. (2015) *Mortgages Made Simple:
Everything You Need to Know about Mortgages.* CreateSpace.

Nadler, M. A. and Rumker, T. (2014) *Real World Personal Finance.*
Lanham: Lexington Books. Available at: http://northumbria.eblib.
com/patron/FullRecord.aspx?p=1727526.

Nadler, M. A. and Rumker, T. E. (2014) *Real world personal finance*. Lanham: Lexington Books.

O'Neil, W. J. (2009) *How to make money in stocks: a winning system in good times or bad*. 4th ed. New York: McGraw-Hill Professional.

Safieddine, F. and Zaharovs, G. (2016) *Buying your first house: England, Wales, Scotland and Northern Ireland*. CreateSpace.

Smith, Ryan (no date) Amazon.co.uk: Books.*BUDGETING: How to manage your money, learn personal finance, get debt free and gain financial freedom (Finance, Personal Finance, Save Money, Goal Setting) eBook:* Available at: https://www.amazon.co.uk/BUDGETING-personal-finance-financial-Personal-ebook/dp/B01GPTN9JI/ref=sr_1_13?s=books&ie=UTF8&qid=1468391694&sr=1-13&keywords=budgeting.

Spencer, P. (2011) *How to buy your first home (and how to sell it too)*. London: Vermilion.

Stevens, J. (2016) *Insurance: best practical guide for risk management, property, liability, life and health with concepts and coverage*. New York: Shepal Publishing.

Taillard, M. (2015a) *Introducing Personal Finance: A Practical Guide*. London: Icon Books. Available at: http://northumbria.eblib.com/patron/FullRecord.aspx?p=1873406.

Missional

Anderson, Ray S. (2001). *The Shape of Practical Theology: Empowering Ministry with Theological Praxis*. Downers Grove, IL: InterVarsity Press,

Anderson, Ray S. (2009). *Re-Jesus: A Wild Messiah for a Missional Church*. Peabody, MA: Hendrickson Publishers, 2009.

Augsburger, David. (2006). *Dissident Discipleship: A Spirituality of Self-Surrender, Love of God, and Love of Neighbor*. Grand Rapids: Brazos Press.

Barrett, Lois, Y. ed. (2003). *Treasure in Clay Jars: Patterns in Missional Faithfulness*. Grand Rapids: Eerdmans,

Boren, M. Scott. (2010). *Missional Small Groups: Becoming a Community that Makes a Difference in the World*. Grand Rapids: Baker,

Briggs, Alan. (2015). *Choosing to Love where God Places You.* The Navigators.

Camp, Lee. C. Mere (2003). *Discipleship: Radical Christianity in a Rebellious World.* Grand Rapids: Brazos Press

Dietterich, Inagrace T. (2006). *Cultivating Missional Communities.* Eugene, OR: Wipf & Stock Publishers,

Fitch, David, Holsclaw, Geoff (2013) *Prodigal Christianity: 10 Signposts into the Missional Frontier.*

Frost, Michael (2011). *The Road to Missional: Journey to the Center of the Church*

Frost, Michael and Alan Hirsch.(2003). The Shaping of Things to Come: Innovation and Mission for the 21st -Century Church. Peabody, MA: Hendrickson Publishers

Frost, Michael, (2015) *Surprise the World: Five Habits of Highly Missional People* -- a great little book that would be useful for a small study group.

Frost, Michael. Exiles: *Living Missionally in a Post-Christian World.* Peabody, MA: Hendrickson Publishers, 2006.

Gibbs, Eddie and Ryan K. Bolger. *Emerging Churches: Creating Christian Community in Postmodern Cultures.* Grand Rapids: Baker Academic, 2005.

Glasser, Arthur F. (2003). *Announcing the Kingdom: The Story of God's Mission in the Bible.* Grand Rapids: Baker Academic,

Gorman, Michael (2011) *Reading Revelation Responsibly: Uncivil Worship and Witness: Following the Lamb into the New Creation*

Green, Hollis L. (2007). *Why Churches Die. Nashville: geaPress.*

Green, Hollis L. (2010). *Discipleship. Nashville: geaPress.*

Green, Hollis L. *(2010). Sympathetic Leadership Cybernetics. Nashville: geaPress.*

Green, Hollis L. *(2010). Why Christianity Fails in America. Nashville: geaPress..*

Green, Hollis L. *(2012). Titanic Lessons. Nashville: geaPress.*

Green, Hollis L. *(2012). Why Wait Till Sunday? Nashville: geaPress..*

Green, Hollis L. *(2013). Fighting the Amalekites. Nashville: geaPress.*

Green, Hollis L. *(2013). Tear Down These Walls. Nashville: geaPress.*

Green, Hollis L. *(2015, 2017). The EVERGREEN Devotional New Testament – C.A.F.E. Edition. Nashville: geaPress.*

Guder, Darrell (2015) *Called to Witness: Doing Missional Theology*, a collection of essays Guder published on the missional church.

Heath, Elaine (2014) *Missional. Monastic. Mainline: A Guide to Starting Missional Micro-Communities in Historically Mainline Traditions*

Hirsch, Alan and Debra Hirsch. (2010) *Untamed: Reactivating a Missional Form of Discipleship*. Grand Rapids: Baker.

Hirsch, Alan and Lance Ford. (2011) *Right Here, Right Now: Everyday Mission for Everyday People*. Grand Rapids: Baker.

Jenkins, Philip. (2002) *The Next Christendom: The Coming of Global Christianity*. New York: Oxford University Press.

Kreider Alan & Eleanor Kreider. (2011) *Worship and Mission After Christendom*. Scottdale, PA: Herald Press.

McNeal, Reggie. (2009) *Missional Renaissance: Changing the Scorecard for the Church*. San Francisco: Jossey-Bass,

Rouse, Rick and Craig Van Gelder. (2008) *A Field Guide for the Missional Congregation: Embarking on a Journey of Transformation*. Minneapolis: Augsburg Fortress

Roxbugh, Alan, Boren, Scott (2009) *Introducing the Missional Church: What It Is, Why It Matters, How to Become One*

Van Gelder, Craig (2007) The Ministry of the Missional Church: A Community Led by the Spirit

Webber, Robert E. (2002) The Younger Evangelicals: Facing the Challenges of the New World. Grand Rapids: Baker.

Wright, Christopher (2006) *The Mission of God: Unlocking the Bible's Grand Narrative* Downers Grove, IL: IVP Academic,

Stewardship

Arrillaga-Andreessen (2012). *Giving 2.0: Transform Your Giving And Our World*. Jossey-Bass. A Wiley Imprint.

Alcorn, Randy. *The Treasure Principle: Unlocking the Secret of Joyful Giving*. Sisters, OR: Multnomah Publishers, Inc., 2001.

Butler, Jason. *Warren Buffett: 23 Simply Amazing Secrets of Warren Buffett for Money Saving, Worthy Investments and Successful Life* Amazon.co.uk: Books 2015. Available at: https://www.amazon.co.uk/Warren-Buffett-Amazing-Investments-Successful- ebook/dp/B01F46CQAQ/ref=sr_1_11?s=books&ie=UTF8&qid=1468391841&sr=1-11&keywords=savings+and+investment.

Christian Smith, Michael O. Emerson. *Passing the Plate: Why American Christians Don't Give Away More Money*. New York: Oxford University Press, 2008.

Christopher, J. Clif. *Not Your Parents' Offering Plate: A New Vision for Financial Stewardship*. Nashville, TN: Abingdon Press, 2008.

Dunnam, Maxie D. *Irresistible Invitation: Responding to the Extravagant Heart of God*. Nashville, TN: Abingdon Press, 2008.

Durall, Michael. *Creating Congregations of Generous People*. Herndon, VA: Alban Institute, 1999.

Felder, Tom. *The Tithing Principle: Understanding Why We Give*. Kansas City: Beacon Hill Press, 2011

Hudnut-Beumler, James. *In Pursuit of the Almighty Dollar: A History of Money and American Protestantism*. Chapel Hill, NC: The University of North Carolina Press, 2007.

Christopher, J. Clif. *Whose Offering Plate Is It? New Strategies for Financial Stewardship*. Nashville, TN: Abingdon Press, 2010.

John Ortberg, Laurie Pederson, Judson Poling. (2000). *Giving: Unlocking the Heart of Good Stewardship*. Grand Rapids, MI: Zondervan.

Kerry Patterson, et. al. *Influencer*. New York: McGraw-Hill, 2008.

Lane, Charles R. *Ask, Thank, Tell: Improving Stewardship Ministry in Your Congregation*. Minneapolis, MN: Augsburg Press, 2006.

LeBlanc, Douglas. *Tithing: Test Me in This*. Nashville, TN: Thomas Nelson, 2010.

Michael Reeves, Jennifer Tyler. *Extravagant Generosity: The Heart of Giving, Program Guide*. Nashville, TN: Abingdon Press, 2011.

Miller, Herb. *New Consecration Sunday Stewardship Program*. Nashville, TN: Abingdon Press, 2007.

Mosser, David N. *The Stewardship Companion: Lectionary Resources for Preaching*. Louisville, K: Westminster John Knox, 2007.

Powell, Mark Allan. *Giving to God: The Bible's Good News about Living a Generous Life*. Grand Rapids, MI: Wm. B. Eerdmans Publishing, 2006.

Robertson, C. K. *Transforming Stewardship*. New York: Church Publishing, 2009.

Ronsvalle, John and Sylvia. *Behind the Stained-Glass Windows*. Grand Rapids, MI: Baker Books, 1996.

Schnase, Robert. *Practicing Extravagant Generosity: Daily Readings on the Grace of Giving*. Nashville, TN: Abingdon Press, 2011.

UK Debt Management Office (no date). Available at: http://www.dmo. gov.uk/.

Wolfe, M. and Madge, P. (2015) *Debt advice handbook*. 11th edition. London: Child Poverty Action Group.

CPSIA information can be obtained
at www.ICGtesting.com
Printed in the USA
JSHW032002051221
20997JS00001B/10